The Book *of* Nocturnes
Philosophical Fragments

Matthew Nini

SPRING PUBLICATIONS
THOMPSON, CONN.

Published by Spring Publications
Thompson, Conn.
www.springpublications.com

© 2025 by Spring Publications and Matthew Nini
All rights reserved
First edition 2025

Produced as part of the project *The Concept of Possibility in Martin Heidegger and in the Wider Context of European Philosophy* (MogMarH) at the Institute of Philosophy, Zagreb, reviewed by the Ministry of Science and Education of the Republic of Croatia and financed through the National Recovery and Resilience Plan 2021–2026 of the European Union—NextGenerationEU.

Cover:

    Raphael
    The Dream of a Knight, c. 1504 (detail)
    National Gallery, London

Typeset in MVB Sirenne

Library of Congress Control Number: 2025946359

ISBN: 978-0-88214-193-0 (paperback)

ISBN: 978-0-88214-194-7 (ebook)

For J.P.L.

Contents

PREFACE 7

PHILOSOPHICAL FRAGMENTS 1–170 13

NOTES 243

PREFACE

Gott spricht zu jedem nur, eh er ihn macht,
dann geht er schweigend mit ihm aus der Nacht.

God speaks to each of us before he makes us, then goes silently with us out of the night. Because we have become artificers, masters of technique, we are under the impression that all things are crafted according to well-lit blueprints. The sleek edges and sharp corners that make up the geometry of the modern city are all drawn with care; the monuments of reason surround us. It is easy to forget that it has not always been this way. The meaning of the old adage, *vita brevis, ars longa* reveals as much: it is not, as one supposes, that art endures while life is fleeting; rather, that art, as what is artificial, the mastery of some technique, takes many lifetimes to master—long enough to forget not only the whole process of discovery, but who we were before we knew, when we stood in wonder before the uses of reason. There is something in us that remains from these days of wonder and ignorance, a deep-seated nature underneath the technical dross. We are illuminated beings, but what is oldest in us is the kernel of darkness beneath the light of art, technique and reason. For reason does not come from reason; light does not beget light. Rather, dawn breaks from darkness; the night is what is older. We rational beings emerge from the night, the time of chaos and irrationality, and step into the dawn.

Works of philosophy are usually books that follow the logic of the day. It is from philosophy that all the modern sciences eventually emancipated themselves. In this way, it holds within itself the origins of the sciences, be they inductive or deductive, concerned with the natural and empirical or the human and subjective. The biologist, the physicist, the mathematician, the philologist, and social scientists of every stripe must proceed impartially and subject their findings to the most rigorous verifications. And to this we owe much. Yet this deployment of reason and its tools into the theatre of life also does it violence. The French term for a naval boarding is *arraisonner*. To reason, *raisonner*, is to forcefully take over, *arraisonner*.

Philosophy, however, is older than any of these particular fields. It contains the seeds of all these sciences within itself, and is exhausted neither by individual scientific disciplines, nor their sum. Part of it, therefore, remains within itself, an obscure part that cannot be subjugated by technique and artifice, because it is a life. This spark of life, which animates all the subsequent technical applications of philosophy, is what the Greeks called *wonder*. Life stands in wonder before itself, and this is the core of the philosophical, the beating heart that cannot be dissected without being stopped.

The place in which the inscrutable beating heart of wonder dwells is called the night. In the night, all the solid shapes of the day are still there, but they are obscured by darkness. The philosophy of night is therefore not opposed to the philosophy of day. It neither rearranges nor destroys. Instead, dim lights allow for new perspectives. In the unfathomable interstices between the objects of reason, fantasies, images, and impossible presences manifest themselves. The Apollonian rule of day—ordered, reasoned, oriented towards the good—is thereby suspended. But the night is not evil. It is merely *what is* before the reasoned journey towards the highest good has been knowingly begun. This, then, is thinking, but not yet reason. Yet because ours is inexorably the standpoint of reason, language, and logic, we can only see the night as reason's precondition; not that which is prior to reason, since reason and the irrational, night and day, are two sides of the same, and come into being together, but that which is older than reason. As the philosopher F.W.J. Schelling writes in his own book of the night, *The Ages of the World*, "Darkness and concealment are the character of the primordial age. All life first forms itself and comes into being in the night. It is for this reason that the ancients called Night the fertile mother of things. Together with Chaos, she is the oldest of all beings."

What sort of book, then, is a philosophical investigation into the meaning of the night? It can only be a paradox, or better still, a riddle. While there are indeed night books, the book itself is fundamentally a day object. Bound in language and constrained by concepts, books and their readers demand an intelligibility that can be subjected to the logic of artifice, the logic of day. If the night, and night-thinking, are to be grasped in language, it must be of a different kind, that of the mythical narrative, the *eikos mythos*. Art, religion, and imaginative story are the oblique paths that lead us into the night. A path is an established connection between one place and another. It always leads to a destination. But if we fix our eyes on the destination, we have abandoned the kind of thinking necessary for the night; to see that far, our eyes must be adjusted to day. As wanderers in the night, we might focus on the path itself, forgetting our point of origin and ignoring our destination. In order to be properly adjusted to our ambitions, writing, the use of language that is always subjected to reasons, must break off before a destination comes into view. Hence our mythical stories will have to be told as fragments.

Beyond the preface, this book is composed of fragments of various length. They are not aphorisms. This point cannot be stressed enough. The Greek *aphorismos* refers to something that has been defined and set apart. It is meant to survive as a whole, the condensation of a principle into its most succinct form. What is enveloped in the aphorism invites being unfolded in commentary: wisdom literature, the domain of the aphorism, calls out for a midrash to apply it to daily life. Here, no midrash is possible because no commentary is necessary—the night is already life in its most intense form. At stake is being able to enter into this life with words without contaminating it with the principles that always stand hidden behind an aphorism. A fragment is merely a text that begins (or at least appears to begin) and does not resolve itself into a conclusion. By definition incomplete, the fragment always has unfinished business.

This book is therefore organized according to just such a fragmentary logic—that is, according to the demands of night-time thinking. The fragments herein are numbered, but their progression is not linear. If one chooses to read them in order, one will find a procession of ideas that moves as a spiral, beginning by articulating a theme, then developing groups of subordinate ideas, and finally linking them more closely, drawing them all in together at the end. It would be better to analyse the structure of the book using the methods of musicology rather than those of literature or philosophy: it is a philosophical sonata with an overture, several themes, their re-articulations in different keys, a coda. But the reader may choose to do otherwise. For while none of the fragments can be considered a completed whole, each stands alone; each is a nocturne in its own key. One can begin at any page, and read in any order. Many fragments do relate to the one that came before it or after it. Some also belong to a series. But these are not necessary relationships. Readers can jump around as they please. The way they connect the constellation of fragments is a kind of composition in its own right; to really read a book is to be its co-author.

Given that books are daytime objects, a book of fragments such as this one is a kind of non-book, or anti-book. While it is primarily a philosophical work, it makes no arguments, and is therefore a non-treatise. It tells stories that go nowhere featuring characters that appear, disappear, and reappear, meaning it is a non-novel as well. It is also a non-history, a non-biography, a non-anthology, and non-poetry. The fragments are a mixture of the refined and unrefined, the integrated and appended. Some of them are merely summaries and interpretations of a single primary text, contributing to another "non-genre" of the book, the non-midrash. Once set in motion, the fragments take on a life of their own, defying both genre and author. And indeed, this non-book has a non-author; it is an unruly self-written book, a graphic *causa sui* into which author and reader are taken up.

Also taken up into the fragments is the book's narrator (or perhaps more fittingly: non-narrator). N***, as we must call him, can only be a hypothesis of the reader. This scholar of night is not to be trusted. He exists only in the margins. Whether the cast of characters that N*** introduces are real, and whether the scholarship N*** presents is reliable, are for the reader to decide. I would advise treating him as you would the hypothetical author of some ancient text: he may or may not exist, and his opinions may or may not be borrowed, exaggerated, or corrupted. More pragmatically, you might think of him as a sort of spirit guide, the Virgil who leads you along disjointed paths as you move through baroque cities, ancient ruins, vast libraries, insomniac nights and improbable encounters. He will help you make the night your own. If some corner of it enthuses you, know that you have likely discovered the mirror image of the piece of night that is your own, the shadow of your daylight self. Be careful, lest it overwhelm you. Some things, dream-like, are best discarded at dawn.

Good night.

Philosophical Fragments

I

Obscure, incomplete, disjointed—night thoughts are shadow riddles, arrested by words, images, sounds, and gestures that are not fully intelligible to us. They speak only in symbols, following a logic that is more ancient than daytime order. A symbol is something broken, snapped in the middle so that it is both itself and something else. It reveals one part—and so there is a night-time logic, one vaguely intelligible to daytime thoughts—but keeps the other hidden. Part of the night is imprisoned within itself, a solid core that we cannot see or understand, but whose presence we feel when we imagine the whole to which it belongs. To venture into the night is to grope for objects, to feel for symbols in the dark and divine their shapes.

2

I remember thee upon my bed. A young woman joined a monastery. During the day, she prayed, worked, and was caught up in the sway of monastic rhythm. But she would wake up in the middle of the night, possessed by a terrible thought: *there is no God.* The thought would send her into a frenzy, and she would sit bolt upright in bed. Then the panic would subside, sleep would return, and dawn would bring renewed piety. But when sleep would no longer come, the terrible thought stayed with her: *there is no God.* When she left the monastery, she could sleep again. In the weeks that followed, she slept long and deeply. The monastic experience had to be transformed in sleep, transmuted into a dream. Once it had achieved this dream-like status, the terribleness of the thought faded away. She is a psychologist now, and has three children. She confessed to me that she does not think much about religion anymore. Perhaps there is a God, she added, but he must be a God of night and dreams.

3

The night is also a sun, proclaims Zarathustra. Day and night are not opposites; still less is night the negation of the day. The night is its own force, and has its own life. Our lives are not divided into the positive of the day and the negative of the night, but rather, two forces are alive in us—Apollo and Dionysius, Ego and Id, night and day.

4

In the Sagrestia Nuova in Florence, four statues, allegories of time, sit two by two atop the tombs embedded into the wall. Michelangelo carved the marble figures of Dawn, Dusk, Day, and Night with a sense of urgency: they contort and move as if they, too, were subject to the passage of time. Night, the most beautiful of the four, reclines with her head on her arm, her muscular body evoking renaissance depictions of Leda, the night mother. Her skin shines like moonlight, and on her brow sits a tiara with crescent moons and a star. Could this star be Saturn, the god of melancholy? Her face is turned downwards, her serenity tinged with sadness. Perhaps before laying down, she ingested some theriac, a potion to soothe her soul, the ingredients for which—poppy seeds—lie at her feet. An owl, figure of both wide-eyed wisdom and darkness, watches over her. Underneath her lies its opposite: an eyeless, hollowed mask, the mask of dreams and opium-inspired fantasy. All things about her marry opposites: this night is both peaceful and restless, wise and mad, strong and frail, ethereal and sensual.

5

More Geometrico. Advice for ethicists: go to bed early, the night is not for you. It is not that the night world is an *immoral* place. Rather, it is an *amoral* place. The logical paths of decision that guide good daytime thinking no longer work at night. When the day looks into the night, it sees blind eroticism, lies, perjury, chaos. It is drawing lines and deducing consequences when it should simply let things *be.* The unique shape of the night, its *Gestalt,* is such that one thing simply comes after another; there is no "because" or "therefore." To juxtapose rather than deduce: this is the Euclidian vision of night.

6

Moving from daytime to night-time reading requires adjusting one's lamp. When read in the wrong light—that is, with the wrong attitude—any book can be made into nonsense. Day books have nothing to tell us when read at night; night books only tell us incomprehensible things when read during the day.

7

Night's accomplices fade away at dawn. The ecstasies that we live in the night—dancing, drunkenness, sex, brotherhood, impassioned discussion—are burned away in morning light. Do we recognize the lover or the friend from the night before when we meet them on the street the next day? Not always.

8

Time marches incessantly around the sundial. Hours and minutes succeed each other, and once elapsed, they can never be retrieved. But the night cannot be measured in the same way. Its main division is into three overlapping infinities: the quiet present, the darkness that surrounds me and goes on forever; the day that has passed, the embers of which fuel the night's events; and the promise of dawn.

9

Perchance to dream. You have heard the speech before:

> To die—to sleep,
> No more; and by a sleep to say we end
> The heart-ache and the thousand natural shocks
> That flesh is heir to: 'tis a consummation
> Devoutly to be wish'd. To die, to sleep;
> To sleep, perchance to dream—ay, there's the rub:
> For in that sleep of death what dreams may come,
> When we have shuffled off this mortal coil,
> Must give us pause—there's the respect
> That makes calamity of so long life.

We think we know what Hamlet says when he makes his dramatic speech: he is saying, shall I go on, or shall I put an end to the whole sordid drama that is life? We moderns love these kinds of reflections, which inevitably begin with the little word "I." But it appears nowhere in Hamlet's speech. He is not engaged in some struggle with sadness, the will of his "I" fighting back an enveloping darkness. No, in his confrontation with the longing for death, Hamlet instead speaks of dreams, and never once says "I." For "I" and my will are not what you think: its shades and nuances are invisible, and are only brought out when we speak and find that we uttered words that are not our own. Are they words that come from dreams? If only it were that easy! For the dream, too, is not what you think. Leave aside your schoolroom allegiances—Freudian, Jungian, Hebrew prophet, tribal shaman, neuroscientist—if you have been looking at the dream as a *something* with which you must wrestle, you have misunderstood it. Dreams are the oldest images, the images that arose before language took its stance as arbiter of interpretation. The dream image swallows up every school of interpretation that seeks to explain it away. The truth of the dream is that there is an image *in* me, *older* than me. The dream represents the radical possibility of interpretation.

10

Ennui, the ugliest of our vices, says Baudelaire. To be ennuied is not simply to be bored, still less to be tired. It is a sort of tiredness that stretches beyond myself, a slurring of the self into the whole, like slurred notes along a musical staff. To be bored is simply to lose one's mental concentration, to widen the aperture of one's spiritual light until it cannot illuminate anything in particular anymore. To be *ennuied* is to rub at the perimeters of the world until they begin to blur.

II

Cities look different at night. Streets that are too familiar become, in the dark, a strange new place. This is the uncanniness of the night. What is uncanny is always a repetition of something familiar, but with a difference. What disturbs is not seeing the double (the city at night, the city in the day), but rather the difference between the two, subtle and unnameable. This city is both the same place and another place at night, *but I cannot say precisely how*. This speaks to the difference in me between the desires I know and those that I cannot yet articulate, that lie just beneath the surface. There is a remainder once I have run through my experience of myself, one that is in me, but so foreign to me that I cannot name it; it is a space of difference that I can never bring to light. This is what makes the wax statue, the parrot, the dark alley, so inexplicably disturbing.

12

Voluptuaries of sleep. Happy people are all alike: they are voluptuaries of sleep. One day is distinguished from another, there is pause and resumption, and things continue where they left off. People who sleep well are always themselves. Insomniacs, however, cannot integrate their experiences into themselves, and remain detached from what they have lived.

13

A thousand-and-one-nights story, as told by Roland Barthes: A mandarin is in love with a courtesan. I will be yours, she says to him, after you have spent a hundred nights waiting for me in the garden under my window. He found a stool and placed it in the garden and each night, observed the light from her window. On the ninety-ninth night, he left with his stool under his arm.

14

If sleep opens up a space for dreams, insomnia opens up one of longing. The insomniac lies in bed and longs for sleep like it were an absent lover. For John of the Cross, the night is the moment when the Soul meets its Beloved: "Upon my flowering breast/Which I kept wholly for Him alone/There He lay sleeping/and I caressing Him/There in a breeze from the fanning cedars." The beloved sleeps, and why not? Night is meant for sleeping. But the lover must continue to desire, continue to watch, to caress, to attend to the beloved, or cease being a lover. Love itself lives in the lover. On the way back from the ball that marks the beginning of their affair, Charlotte says to Werther, close your eyes and sleep like the others in the carriage with us. Werther answers, "As long as I see these eyes open... there is no danger." Charlotte proposes that Werther be the beloved, but he will not have it: he longs for longing. In the end, the longing becomes greater than the subject, and it engulfs the one who does the longing. The question, then, is not, what do I think about in my insomnia? But rather, what thinks in me when I cannot sleep? Or better still, what drama is being played out in me when I cannot sleep?

15

For much of his career, Freud thought that our drives, the longings that sustain the movement of life, belonged only to Eros. To be alive is to live an erotic existence. Later, Freud would separate the forward-moving sex drive from the backward moving death drive. Consciousness has a deep memory—a bodily, somatic memory—of what it was before. Our deepest past stretches back not only into the evolutionary history of the mammals that we are, but back into the sea: to the life of amphibians and tetrapods, sponges and fungi, back to stromatolites at the border between mineral and animal life. The Ancients, both Christian and Pagan, wrote Lapidaries, long poems that describe the hidden properties of precious stones, which had both medicinal and religious uses. Freud's Lapidary would be one of elements: carbon, hydrogen, nitrogen, oxygen, phosphorus, and sulphur, the things in which we live and move and have our being, to which we all return in death. Caught in the strife of eros, the body longs for elemental bliss: the return to the homeostasis of the inorganic. Our deep past is our deep future: it is the peace of mineral sleep.

16

Voluptuaries of sleep II. It is easy to retro-read our modern sleeping habits into history, and see it as divinely ordained: God separated the day from the night, the day is for working, and the night is for resting. This is then codified in Saint Benedict's rule—*Ora et labora*: a day is constituted of eight hours of prayer, eight hours of work, and eight hours of sleep. But Benedict did not mean this separation to bl e so rigid; there were times of prayer in the night, and times for rest and recreation in the day. More than to the monastery, we owe the stark separation of night and day to the factory owners of the Industrial Revolution: as long as there is light, there is work; when the light has gone out, you should rest so you can go back to work when the light returns. Here, the night belongs to the day, sleep is robbed of its eros, and with Thanatos reigning as hierophant, we begin to fear sleep as we once feared death: insomnia is for moderns. The sleep of the ancients was polyphasic—a first sleep early in the night, and a second sleep in the early morning are separated by a period of nocturnal activity. There are two nights: a night for sleeping, and a night for keeping watch, and two days: a day for working and a day for slumbering.

17

In Rome, my apartment is across the street from a mechanic's workshop. The mechanic and I drink coffee together after lunch at the café next door. Then he returns to his apartment above the shop and sleeps for an hour, sometimes more. *The Romans know that the real sleep, the deep sleep, is the afternoon sleep,* he tells me. I stay in the café and read until the noonday heat has passed.

18

Sleep is eros as well, the pleasure that is the caesura between days. Who has not, to use a Proustian image, buried their cheeks into the soft cheeks of a pillow, sinking into easy pleasure? But perhaps this is not so easy: to sleep is to move out of oneself, to move beyond the consciousness of daytime. In this, sleep is more like making love than any so-called easy pleasure: to fall asleep is to merge into something greater than oneself, just as the climactic moment of love-making is a shared moment of pleasure not where two become one, but where both become something else, a third thing that lasts only a moment. This fleeting moment, whether somnolent or orgasmic, is a *petite mort*, a little death that fades into oblivion. The medieval physician thought that every orgasm shortened one's lifespan. The thought is a refrain in the poems of John Donne, for whom a peaceful death, sleep, and the parting of lovers all belong to the same movement: "As virtuous men pass mildly away,/And whisper to their souls to go,/Whilst some of their sad friends do say/The breath goes now, and some say, No:/So let us melt, and make no noise,..."

19

The witching hour. The time between the first and second sleep is an unusual one. Night thoughts prevail. Monks are awake then, praying the psalms, their night vigil both monotonous and fearful, between death and waking. They are to prevent the witching hour—both in the modern sense of counteracting it with their prayers, and in the old sense of preceding it, *praevenio*. For at three o'clock, the witches begin their rituals. Their spells induce the second sleep. Following our circadian rhythms, it is the deepest sleep: the time of nightmares, sleepwalking, paralysis. The monks pray that we will survive the evil hour, and that dawn will come for us once again.

20

Few experiences are richer than slowly coming to oneself in the grey hours just before dawn. This is the gloomy moment that Philip Larkin calls "soundless dark": "In time the curtain-edges will grow light. / Till then I see what's really there..." The room around me is ambivalent, the very being of the things that make up my world is unstable. The relation between subject and object is also unstable. This room, these objects, these sensuous experiences are not *mine*, as they are during the day, but somehow a patchwork of being into which I can insert myself in myriad ways. In the opening pages of Proust's *In Search of Lost Time*, the narrator, after falling asleep over his bed-time reading, has the impression of perhaps *being* the things he was reading about; in the waxing and waning of sleep he is transformed into "a church, a quartet, the rivalry between François I and Charles V." Time and space are out of joint. We have all had this experience of being suspended between sleeping and waking, with objects slowly taking shape as consciousness returns. The sleeper wakes up in his grandparents' house, long demolished, in his old school, or in some faraway place. He is simultaneously child and adult, what he was and what he is. Objects are transformed: heaps of pillows become old lovers, or vast expanses of cloud stuff; the door frame becomes a Rodin sculpture; the lamp a small mythical beast; the coat rack an old man. Then one returns to oneself, things solidify, and two states of affairs—the room and me on the one hand, the room and my fantasies on the other—part ways. It is dawn, and things are solid again.

21

Melancholia. In a text of disputed authenticity, Aristotle (or pseudo-Aristotle, as the case may be), wonders why so many of the "great men"—among them Empedocles, Plato, Socrates, and almost all of the poets—are of an "atrabilious temperament." To be *atrabilious* is to suffer from a surfeit of black bile. Its color, black, *melas* in Greek, yields a mood, a feeling tone, an ambience, a lugubrious music that saturates the room. This mood is the child of Greek tragic madness, of Euripides's Herakles, driven mad by a goddess so that he would kill his own children, and of Platonic frenzy, the *theia mania* of priests, poets and lovers, possessed by a god. It is "the clouding of consciousness, depression, fear and delusions, and finally, the dreaded lycanthropy, which drove its victims through the night as howling, ravening wolves," which to the ancient mind "were all regarded as effects of the sinister substance whose very name, *melas*, conjured up the idea of all that was evil and nocturnal." Melancholy is a madness that comes from the will being overwhelmed by the divine. Even in the old Greek literature, it can only exist as a paradox: mad Herakles has strength that fails him when he is sane; the poet who has learned his craft can only sing when his will cedes to the muses. There are melancholy diseases—epilepsy, paralysis, depression, phobias, ulcers—that a surge in black bile might cause in any of us. And there are those whose disposition is marked by melancholy. The natural melancholic, the *melankholikos dia phusin*, is also prone to creative excitement, lest he become all too melancholic, and cede to lethargy, convulsions, and dyspepsia. The depressive bodily effect of black bile removes the boundaries imposed by the will, and excites the mind. Just as wine, a depressive, removes inhibitions and creates a kind of frenzy, melancholy creates a state of nervous tension and excitation. Melancholy is a form of intoxication, the *ivresse* of Baudelaire, and causes a *vis imaginativa*: the failing memory and hyperactive imagination of the melancholic can lead to phantasmagoric excess; his past sinks into oblivion, and his dreams become prophesies. The poet who sings the lives of the heroes as if they were images from his own dreams steps out of our world and onto the plains of Troy or the shores of Ithaca.

22

Clock-watching is the insomniac's worst habit. I go to bed early and fall asleep—or almost, I'm never quite sure—and a half hour later, I come out of the lull of tiredness, and wonder what time it is. Trains, less and less frequent, are heard in the distance. The night grows deeper. *One o'clock.* There is still hope for a good night's sleep. *Two o'clock.* The deep stillness is soothing, there is time for at least a little rest. *Three o'clock,* the witching hour. Now agitation sets in. Once it passes, sleep may come. But by four, my hope has turned towards dawn. There is a change in the light. Soon others will awake, there will be movement downstairs somewhere, and knowing that others have set about the tasks of daily life brings me comfort; the world is working again, others have slept, they are ready to look after me if this sleeplessness is really some sickness, and the thought of being looked after brings comfort. It saves me from the unfamiliar shapes of the morning-gray world. Sleep comes, but too late, like a lover who arrives and says there is no time left for dinner, no time left for the theater, just a little walk before we part again.

23

Perchance to dream II. My dreams are mine, but am I the one doing the dreaming, or does someone dream in me? And perhaps this other is not only in me, but also beyond me— *interior intimo meo, superior summo meo*. The reader will protest: of course my dreams are mine, they take place in my mind, they are my private mental imagery. But dreams are not so simple. They are our personal mythology; not the story we tell ourselves, but the stories we receive as if from a distant source. Or better still: they are our personal epics. In my dream, I am the primeval author—Homer, poet before poetry, man outside of history—and in this sense, completely unknown to myself. But I am also Odysseus, the man of many turns, the *polytropos*, the wise hero of my own tale, confronted with the fantastic, the sporadic, and the irrational. My Homeric dream-making self has answers, but no questions. My Odyssean dreaming self has questions, but no answers. These two cannot simply be put together and solved like the Sphinx's riddle. There is a tension between these two facets of my dreaming self, and it is precisely the tension between them that is the energy, the *eros* of the dream. Bring them together, and you do not solve the mystery of the dream: you simply wake up.

24

I*** recounts how his struggles with insomnia began. He had flown from Rome to Tokyo, and after three days there, flew on to Vancouver. When he landed, he stumbled into his hotel room in an exhausted daze, and collapsed onto the bed. But he could not sleep. The trip through innumerable time zones, across constellations, to lands where the firmament is arranged differently, created a kind of existential confusion that lodged itself in his body. He had been robbed of night.

25

Ibn Butlan, the greatest physician of eleventh century Baghdad, was much translated in medieval Europe, and there are remarkable illustrated Latin editions of his treatise on health, *Tacuinum Sanitatis*. His admonitions on sleep are characteristic of his time: one sleeps best between the first and last hours of the night (a vague remark); its nature is to immobilize the senses, to warm the body, and to hydrate it; yet too much sleep can ruin one's digestion, especially if one sleeps on an empty stomach. It is best, then, to sleep after eating something moist (*cum cibis humectantibus*). Sleep is a remedy for the phlegmatic or melancholic (*flegmaticis alias melencolicis*) and the elderly, regardless of the climate in which they find themselves. The illustration of sleep in the fifteenth century Rhineland manuscript of the *Tacuinum* I have before my eyes at the National Library of Paris shows a sleeper in a bonnet, tucked into bed, head over hand over pillow. The sheets are tussled, the sleeper is restless, perhaps ill. A musician plays a lullaby on a lute. A bedpan is visible, ready to receive what is left of the *cibis humectantibus*.

26

The night is not the day's other. To think so is to remain in the logic of the day, the logic of dialectic. Clever ethicists have convinced us that everything is a dialectic of *I* and *you*. Clever theologians ride on their coat tails and try to convince us that there is a still-higher dialectic of *I* and *Thou*. The theologians have understood the game: a dialectic always proceeds to a higher level until it has swallowed everything up. But do not be fooled by these old pedants: dialectic can only return to where it began. We must think differently. Day's becoming night and night's becoming day is not the surrender to an Other. The two are together, but forever two. It is precisely the tension that arises from their twoness that creates the vitality that allows them to be a living One. Neither two-in-one, nor one-in-two, their opposition creates their unity. This is the living friction of concepts that only occurs in the dark, and that dialectic will always try to smooth out.

27

P*** recounts his visit to the Capuchin catacombs in Palermo. Row upon row of mummified corpses along the walls greet the visitor. *Once again, the South makes clear its fascination with the underworld.* P*** is from the North, the Italy of day-thoughts. Here in the catacombs, amidst night-shapes and night-poses, thinking plays a different role. *The tranquillity that surrounds you,* he says to me. *No depressing thoughts.*

28

And why should the night induce depressing thoughts? The night is a time when limit and limitless, finite and infinite, boundaries and their transgressions, are all blurred. There is only the night-shape, the silhouette, and its living meaning—that is, what it becomes as it is acted out. The image and its coming-forth, shadow and ecstasy: those are the truest night thoughts.

29

Keep watch. Not only monks make vigils. Whenever something momentous happens, it is preceded by a sleepless night of the soul, a holding not only of one's breath, but of one's whole existence before the event overwhelms and swallows everything. Gethsemane is the model, that night of sweat and blood before the crucifixion. But thinkers of the day have too often concentrated on the wilful, subjective elements of this moment: stay alert, says the spiritual author, do not abandon the lord like the disciples. Keep watch. This misses the point entirely. To keep watch is to open oneself up into a space of watchfulness, an easy wakefulness that is a waiting for something unknown. It was during the second watch of the night—that is, at the witching hour—that Siddhartha achieved enlightenment. The Buddha also had his Gethsemane.

30

In a Viennese café, early evening. A man, dishevelled, thin, looking half-mad, sits down in one of the booths and orders a glass of beer. He produces from his bag an enormous notebook, opens it at the middle, and begins writing on the blank pages. His script is thick and rune-like, strong black lines decorated with arabesques. As I glance over his shoulder, hidden, I cannot decipher anything. What language is this? Perhaps it is no language at all, but a kind of hieroglyph meant only for the gods. He writes slowly. It must have taken him a long time—perhaps his whole life up until now—to fill the first half of the book with his mysterious script. A childlike thought occurs to me: if he has been writing for his whole life, when did he learn this elaborate alphabet? There in the café, where all boundaries faded away with the weak light of the table lamps, the answer was simple: *Before.*

31

Via Giulia, in a shady side street along the Tiber, thick with buildings and arcs dating back to Julius II, the most extravagant of Popes. Through a tall gate and into a muddy courtyard, up a stone staircase worn by five centuries of feet, up the narrow stairwell lined with thin and dirty ancient bricks, we peek through a door left ajar. Ingeborg Bachmann is not concerned with closing doors properly. Her thoughts are splayed out over the entire city. The fiery afternoon light carries her to the Roman Forum, and she stands at the temple of Vesta next to Goethe, surveying the ruins. He says to her, do you not find that the statue of Marcus Aurelius in the city is a perfect representation of Don Giovanni? And she notices that the cigarette has fallen out of her mouth, and she reaches over to the coffee table for a new one. This search for a new cigarette brings her attention to the divan directly across, where Ludwig Wittgenstein, his hair a mess and his shirt collar open, sits next to his brother Paul, who is anxiously rubbing the stump that once was his right hand. Ludwig begins to whistle the Commendatore's aria from Don Giovanni in a clear, bright tone. The notes were so perfectly articulated that she began to mouth the words she had heard at the Teatro dell'Opera a few weeks before: *Don Giovanni, a cenar teco...* Don Giovanni, you have invited me to dine. She decides that she needs a barbital tablet, and as she struggles to free it from the packaging, the cigarette falls out of her mouth for a second time. She reaches for the glass of whiskey on the low table next to her, and sees that Hugo von Hofmannsthal stands near the window, inspecting the inner courtyard. He turns to direct a sidelong glance at her, severe and melancholic. Old Vienna, with all its pretence and eccentricity, its kitsch and black humour, has descended upon her Roman hideout. Paul Wittgenstein now begins to sing Don Giovanni's serenade, *Deh vieni alla finestra,* oh come to the window. Hofmannsthal turns around, taking offense at the singing. Ludwig is still whistling the Commendatore scene, and is coming to the dramatic parts. His facial expression shows extreme concentration. The cacophony the brothers produce is unbearable. Between her and the Wittgenstein brothers, thin wisps of smoke begin to rise. Ethereally, half-hidden in the smoke, Goethe reappears, standing behind the Wittgensteins. He speaks in a strong voice that drowns out the warring music below him: *Why, then, all this pain and yearning? Sweet peace, come, oh come into my breast!* She looks at the men around her, and sees their legs being kissed by flames. "So it ends in a farce," she says.

32

Do you want to see how inadequate ethics is for night-thinking? Then think of Antigone. Her brother has been killed in battle. The gods of the city require that the betrayer's body rot in the sun. But the chthonic gods, the gods of the night, require that he be returned to the earth. Antigone, the sister, the woman, has an uncanny attachment to the earth gods; to earth, womb, and darkness, the places before the beginning and after the end. No daylight patriarch can know the bond between the womb and the earth. In the wake of Antigone's burial of her brother Polyneices, a long series of unwitting deaths occur. Creon, the King, orders Antigone be buried alive. He then has a change of heart, but she hangs herself before he can intervene. His son Haemon, in love with Antigone, kills himself. When she learns of her son's death, Queen Eurydice kills herself, too. Creon's one-sided allegiance to the day, to the city, to the world above, brought about the end of his house. He is left to lament the cruelty of the Fates. But the emptiness of his house speaks more about the fullness of the earth than the power of the city. What power did the city have other than to annihilate itself? Creon's error was to observe the gods of the earth only from the highest citadel. Seek to suppress the night, and you will suffer—at sunset, all will be consumed.

33

Cardinal Richelieu prayed every other day, or rather, every other night. Two hours before midnight, he would open his breviary, the prescribed prayers meant to punctuate the day, and pray all the hours before midnight. After midnight, he would pray all the hours for the next day.

34

Melancholia II. The form that melancholy adopts in the Middle Ages emphasizes its paradoxical nature. *Acedia* is identified with the sin of sloth, but is in fact a kind of holy boredom. It is an "aversion and anxiety of the heart" (*taedium sive anxietatem cordis*), which makes one seek out distraction. The monk, confined to his monastery, going from his cell to the refectory to the chapel to the field and back to his cell in an unending cycle rhythmed by the same bells and the same chants, wishes he were anywhere else than where he is. This constant desire of flight, foreshadowing the romantic *Wanderlust*, is coupled with the need to be busy: only distractions will cure the boredom, only action, however meaningless, can be a reprieve from the emptiness of contemplation. This agitation is called the noonday devil, since it strikes during the long afternoons of the monastic day. Its combination of restlessness and lethargy incarnates the paradox of melancholy in daytime tones: it is a desiring of desire, a longing for an object that cannot be identified. And indeed, any object will do. It is not until the monk fights the desire to flee and remains in his cell that he can come to terms with the source of the problem—*himself.*

35

For Karl Jaspers, our existence is divided into laws of the day and passions of the night. The day, the place of ambitions and measurements, grand projects and conquests, falls through when the sun sets. Then, eroticism, betrayal, violence, and irrepressible desires arise. The demon that we have spurned calls at sunset. But for Jaspers, night turns into day, and day into night, until night is taken up into day: the chthonic gods are swallowed up and become a disposition, a *Gemüt*, of the one God—his wrath. Jaspers goes to bed early and sleeps. Emil Cioran also goes to bed early, but cannot sleep. The remainder, the foundational abyss of night that Jaspers had tried to argue away, becomes cruelly present for Cioran. And he is afraid to miss its arrival. Nights when we have slept, he writes, are nights that did not exist. Only the sleepless night, the white night, the *nuit blanche*, speaks to us. Jaspers attempted to integrate day into night by means of dialectic, the metaphysician's trick. Cioran stares at it with wide daylight eyes—his night is a day with no sun.

36

Is my little book pedantic? Yes. I cannot sleep, I read at night, I scour libraries during the hot afternoons to feed my nightly compulsions. But there is no reason for you to read what I have read. If I am of any help at all, it is only in creating the conditions for your own thinking. Let the night work on you, and have your own thoughts.

37

Let our patron as night-thinkers be the figure found on the first tarot card—or the card before the first, the card given the number 0, the Magician. The French say it better (and isn't the tarot from Marseilles?): he is the juggler, the *bateleur*. His depiction on the card describes who he is. The young man wears a hat shaped liked a figure eight. He stands in front of a small table. On the table are a yellow vase; seven disks, three red and three yellow; two dice; a knife; a bag. He holds a rod in his right hand, a ball in his left. These are play things, but to succeed at these games requires the utmost concentration. Yet it is not the severe concentration of work, but the easy concentration of play. To keep the disks in the air, the juggler must be entirely focused on the task, but not overthink it. For ruminating brings one away from the rhythm of juggling, from the easy playfulness of act. Do you wish to think night-thoughts? Then learn to concentrate without effort.

38

Pessimism belongs to the day. The pessimist stares into the night, looking for an object with which the pupils can engage. He opens his eyes ever wider, trying to see something, even if he knows that there is nothing to see. With every blink, he celebrates his own realism—they can't fool me, he says, I know that there's nothing there. The pessimist's blank stare will only give him a headache. To see in the night, one needs owl eyes. Illuminating the night to see what is there will only result in a surfeit of brightness, in which one cannot see—a *nuit blanche*. One must train one's eyes to be like those of the beast that sees in starlight.

39

Restless legs. The eponymous protagonist of Paul Leppin's "Prague ghost novel" *Severins Gang in die Finsternis* (1914) leads a half-rapturous, half-insipid life. Much like Kafka's Josef K. (in *The Trial*), Severin works in a dreary office where bad air and bad company have deleterious effects on his health. He returns home in the afternoon exhausted, collapses on a divan, and sleeps until the lamps are lit. Then, when the streets of Prague are transformed by the play of stone and shadow, he rises and walks the city. Compulsively, anxiously, pushed forward by some invisible force of obsession, he wanders, going from park to tavern to seedy night cafés, never stopping for long. Born a generation too late, Severin still has a consumptive air about him; he would have made a good romantic: twenty-three and a university dropout, he is devoured by obsessions he cannot name. His wanderings lead him into abandoned chapels, dilapidated cemeteries, hidden drinking dens, and the beds of strange women. From the vast expanses of the gothic cathedral to the narrow streets of the Jewish quarter, from basement brothels to the attic of the Old Synagogue where the Golem is hidden, his Prague is a place of spent passions and decrepitude, "a haunted city full of nocturnal miracles and glowing lanterns, afraid of the light of day."

40

What the Church Fathers called *acedia*, Pascal calls *divertissement*. "All the misery of man comes from one thing," he writes, "not knowing how to remain quietly in a room." Why do armies march across borders, why do seducers pursue unattainable women, why does the moneylender hoard gold? To these enormities, Pascal offers the simplest of answers: boredom. His hyperbole rolls unbounded through the imagination: stay in your room, learn to be at home with yourself, lest you join the ranks of Pyrrhus who sought to conquer all of Europe. Pascal's is a night cure to day problems: stay in your room, the place where you sleep, where you wait for darkness to subside, and travel through the dreamland of your imagination, a place as wild and exaggerated as the stories of Rabelais, as infinite as the hyperbole of boredom.

41

A young Dane arrives in Paris. His name is Malte, and his story (at least at first) is easy to follow. He is the last of a long line of Danish nobility. The sale of the family's estate has allowed him to live comfortably, moving from one European capital to another. He is a poet, and has come to the City of Light to exercise his craft. But it is here where Malte's story begins to break down. *The Notebooks of Malte Laurids Brigge,* Rainer Maria Rilke's so-called experimental novel, does not have a plot, and despite the impression given in its first pages, it has neither setting nor character either. Malte's Paris is not the City of Lights, but rather one of darkness, a place of poverty, sickness, and filth. The young poet can only see Paris through the prism of Baudelaire, an image formed before he arrived. He not only wanders through the city as if through a narrow dreamscape, his feelings about it blur the lines between sight and seen, subject and object, first and third person. It is not that the city and its darkness bring him out of himself; rather, his own subjectivity is blurred, merging with the urban fresco. Friendless, Malte observes the world not from the outside, but with the slightly displaced point of view that nightmares, opium, or agony provide. The world of stable things, the Apollonian universe of culture, religion, state, and identity are called radically into question. Malte does not ask "who am I?" as much as: "who is this I who stands out from the parade of things that come and go?" The impressionistic stories of the *Notebooks* are sketches in which the narrator becomes entirely consumed: he is not only the man having an epileptic fit, but the epilepsy itself, a strange rapturous dance; he not only remembers the agony of his grandfather, he is the laboured breathing and the spectre of death. Rilke's poetic ability to have a narrator dissolve his identity and inhabit an experience transgresses the limits that are normally required for those experiences to emerge. While this takes on a nightmarish hue as one reads, its result—if one can follow it all the way to the end—is the serenity of a freedom that is self-aware. But to achieve this serenity, we must pass through all the states that disturb the solidity of self-consciousness, whether liminal (dreaming), somatic (convulsive fits), or intellectual (the concentration of the reader; the ecstasy of the imagination). One finds a microcosm of this procedure in the sketch wherein Malte recounts his childhood games of playing dress-up. Changing costumes and looking at himself in the mirror does not lead to a disturbance in identity, but rather the consolidation of one around the many forms it can take: "These disguises, though, never went so far as to make me feel a stranger to myself; on the contrary, the more complete my transformation, the more convinced I was of my own identity." But the young thespian's belief in the credibility of his own characters falters when he walks into a table on the way to the mirror and scatters the trinkets that were on it. He catches a sidelong glance of himself, the actor, not playing a role, but failing to play one, and destroying some real arrangement of things in the world thereby. Malte's world is not one in which order degenerates into chaos, but rather, in which the consistent and believable roles of play-acting cover up something more primitive, and that, from the standpoint of the world stage, looks chaotic and destructive. The most real things seem dream-like only because of the limitations of self-consciousness. Make a real existential move, make a *decision,* and it will always have a Dionysian, chaotic, irreducible element that self-consciousness cannot grasp.

42

Perchance to dream III. Let me tell you my dream. Not so easy, since dreams often dissipate with first light. But as the dream enthusiast will tell you, the more one pays attention to one's dream life, the easier it is to recall them. This is not some sudden act of will, but a creative (or better still: re-creative) process. The stage on which it unfolds is the recording of dreams. When we write down our dreams, we subject them to a discursive process that is alien to their original form. In Platonic terms, the dream is pure vision, a *noesis,* but the written dream is discursive, *dianoia.* The transferring of the dream material from the one form to the other is just as significant as the moment of dreaming. For whether one writes it down or merely retells it to oneself, one is bringing the most primordial element of the night—the *massa confusa* of images that emerges when the self fades into torpor—into the day. This is such a violent jolt that the dream seems to resist: it wants to stay in the night.

43

Do not follow my bad example: you will not become a thinker by overmuch reading. You must not let the Doctors and the Pharisees who write books think for you.

44

Melancholia III. It is the alchemists and doctors of early modernity who best incarnate the paradox of melancholy. Their madcap writings, aimed at diagnosing and cataloguing melancholy, abound with contradictory details. Here, one should refer to Robert Burton's seventeenth century masterwork, *The Anatomy of Melancholy*. More than an eccentric medical treatise, it is an open-ended system, both a complete work of science and a game, a transformation of all of human experience into a literary puzzle whose solution is found through adopting the mood—melancholy—that allows one to play the game. Begin on any page, start reading, and if you have adopted the right disposition, you will be able to enter into the system and navigate it with the easy concentration of a real night-thinker. I open the book to a random page: diet as cause of melancholy. Here, one must understand that in the *Anatomy*, nearly everything causes melancholy, just as nearly everything can cure it. Beef, goat's flesh, hart and deer, all venison, hare, conies, ducks, geese, swans, herons, and pigeons are all meats of melancholy. Of vegetables, cucumbers, melons, cabbage, and all greens, being "windy vegetables" are suspect. Root vegetables and fruits, especially apples, pears, plums and cherries, are all forbidden to the melancholic. Spices, bread from dark grains, wines and any thick drink, are all atrabilious. Later, Burton will change his mind about wine, apples, and spices. Only carp, "a fish of which I know not what to determine," remains eternally neutral. Love can be a cure for certain species of melancholy, but can also be its own kind of sadness, love-melancholy. Sleeping and waking, retention and evacuation, sport and leisure, are all alternately cause and cure. This ruse of language is both the cause and cure of Burton's own melancholy. Only in writing about it can he rise up from the depths of depression and into imaginative frenzy. This is because melancholy is the soul's rejection of the laws of the day, all while affirming the need for day-language. Melancholy occurs at twilight hours. It is, among other things, a consequence of the inadequacy of concepts. The nonconceptual nature of the mood that is melancholy forces Burton to write it into existence. But as soon as the words are put to paper, they reveal themselves to be inadequate. Since there is no concept to which one can return, no means of starting over, one can only write more. This is the genius of melancholy: it has no beginning and no end.

45

To be enthralled by one's experience, to belong to it, to move within it—that is what is at stake.

46

Most lives have been lost to history. People are born and then disappear, bringing their achievements and their stories with them into oblivion. How many billions of people have been utterly forgotten? The arrival of the written word changed this. Writing inaugurates not only what we call history, but a kind of immortality; spoken words disappear into the wind, but writing stays—*verba volant, scripta manet*. Some modern writers have pushed the possibility of writing's gravitational force to its limit, recording the minutiae of days in diaries, fixing every thought in ink. In the hands of scholars, this has given rise to the age of the critical edition: every scribbling of every writer is edited and published. Only thoughts remain really private, and this because of their sheer ephemerality—like clouds, thoughts float away and disperse. But the proliferation of diaries and critical editions, the opening of the archives, has made writing itself into something ephemeral. Perhaps the great polymaths of the seventeenth century were still able to read everything, but we have so much to read that each of us will die having read virtually *nothing*. The total identification of life with the written record thereof exhausts the idea of writing, and propels us into a new kind of forgetting: not the days before writing, but after it. Now, what is noteworthy is not what has not been archived, but the gap in the written record—paradoxically, a remembered forgetting. While the modern life lived but not recorded is, superficially, the opposite of the recorded events of antiquity (one written about, one not), each occupies the same place in their respective systems. But there is a higher level still, an even more sophisticated rapport between life and writing: the life that is recorded, but never shared. It was long thought that the Egyptian hieroglyphs were a form of writing only for the gods, only intelligible to a few priests and the mysterious god for whom they were intended. The sealed archive, the inaccessible record (or even better: the text whose very existence is unknown) is just such a message to the gods— a secret commerce, a silent dialogue.

47

When Dante arrives in hell, he meets the strange figure of Guido da Montefeltro, who tells his story as a private confession to the poet, happy to unburden himself of the long narrative. He speaks freely because he believes that Dante will never leave hell; his story should be a secret to the living. Dante, who is on an odyssey through hell and heaven, is therefore a sort of spiritual voyeur. What Montefeltro shows us is that the essence of confession is to speak something that will never be repeated. Augustine and Rousseau, whose introspection is meant for a broad readership, are really making anti-confessions. The secret writing of the diarist, the priestly hieroglyphics that we once attributed to the Egyptians, and the letter-burning author are all making real confessions. The true confession must be both said and unsaid, made and destroyed: its embers are already a kind of forgiveness.

48

Athens, the most unsavory of neighborhoods. I was walking after dinner, in the evening cool. On the ground floor of a tall concrete building along my way was a little tavern. I went in, sat at a table, ordered wine, and lit a cigarette. Behind the counter stood an old, tired-looking woman in black. She brought my carafe and crossed the empty bar to return to her glasses and bottles. An older man came in, sat down at the counter, and ordered wine. Another came and did the same. They sat a seat apart, and did not talk to each other, but rather both spoke to the old woman without looking at each other. A clicking of heels. From a door to my left, across from the entrance, emerged a young woman in a black dress, her dark hair flowing as she moved. She sat between the men, and the conversation became more jovial. Then she stood and returned to where she had come from. After a moment, the first man paid for his drink and went out through the door from which the woman had come. More young girls and more old men came, going in and out the two doors. While I saw the girls re-emerge from the door on the left, I never saw a man return from there. They came in through the man entrance, followed a girl through the door to the left, and never returned. By now it was late, and the waitress told me that I could rent a room for the night if I wished. I paid for the wine and went out the main entrance on the right.

49

The philosopher's secret. You must understand that every word, every action, every decision of yours is the product of a dialogue. There are two in you: one who speaks and one who listens; one who acts and one who is acted upon; one who knows and one who learns. When the philosophers tell you, I am wise because I know I do not know, they are only telling you half the truth. The other half is: I am also wise because I do not know that I know, and that I have possessed this unrecognized knowledge from the beginning.

50

An old legend states that the Golem, the monstrous creature brought to life by Rabbi Lev to protect the Jews of Prague, is hidden in the attic of the Old-New Synagogue. Despite many attempts, I have never been allowed into this attic, nor does anyone I know report having been themselves. This shows, perhaps, that one can find anything in Prague, but should not necessarily go looking for it.

51

I remember thee upon my bed II. I***'s continuing battle with insomnia provoked deeply religious experiences. He thought that after getting back from Vancouver, he would return to normal cycles of sleep and wakefulness. But his night had been robbed from him. He lay in bed and sleep would not come. Instead came anxiety, the most primordial anxiety, angst about life and death. In those hours of dread, he began to talk to God not only in the most Christian way, but with the most perfect understanding of the abyss that non-being opens up. "Lord, come to me in my suffering. Let me accompany you in yours. We will sit together in the garden and keep watch, and I will join my sleeplessness to yours, and mix my blood with yours." These cries from the abyss would cease when first light broke. I*** awoke, shaved, dressed, combed his hair, went to his office, was never melancholic, and never thought about God. But in his bed in the dark, people and voices arose each night that were completely real for him, and his faith was completely authentic. He had become a night-disciple; bad at making converts, but good at keeping watch.

52

There is a beautiful German word that describes the waxing and waning of light, equally applicable to sunrise and sunset: *Dämmerung*. The *Dämmerung* is a moving in-between, a place that is already but not yet. One is enveloped by light that is faint in its beginning or ending, is possessed by it, transformed by it, and just before the experience reaches its apogee, it is over. This is a liminal experience, a short balancing that cannot be sustained. Sleepwalking, daydreaming, trance, contemplation—these are the manifestations of the *Dämmerung*.

53

Sleepwalking is a *Dämmerung* of the soul. It is the body's way of imitating the juggler-magician, of reaching a kind of easy concentration. In the motley collection of learning that is the *General Collection of Discourses of the Virtuosi of France* (1664), one of the virtuosi exclaims that he "wonder'd not so much to see a man walk in his sleep... but (indeed) how they perform'd their actions better in the night than in the day, and with more courage, and wake not during those violent motions and stirrings." The Romantics were taken up with the same idea. The liminal world of sleepwalking was a space of creativity, where imagination was given license to do what it wished, unrestrained by moral conscience and logical understanding. Kleist's *Prince of Homburg* (1809–10) begins with the Prince exhausted after a long battle. He sleeps, and then, in an intense somnambulist experience, is coerced by his peers to declare his love for the niece of the Elector of Brandenburg, Natalie, and takes one of her gloves. Upon waking, he is puzzled by the mysterious glove. When the Prince learns during the next day's war council that the glove is Natalie's, he is so shaken that he does not hear the orders given to him: stay your regiment, do not attack. When the enemy arrives at Fehrbellin, he charges, and miraculously, is victorious. The Somnambulist prince was maintained in his liminal state through an uncanny realization: his dreams had been more efficacious than reason.

54

In "The Facts in the Case of M. Valdemar" (1845), perhaps Edgar Allen Poe's most disturbing story, a mesmerist, learned in the obscure theories of animal magnetism and vitalism, hypnotizes a dying man. The dying Valdemar's agitation is such that he seems caught between trance and lucidity, breathing and speaking, reporting that he is already dead. Although he was meant to die within two days, Valdemar lives seven more months in this hypnotic state, at which point he asks his hypnotist to make a decision: wake him or put him back to sleep. As the mesmerist brings his patient out of his trance, Valdemar cries "Dead! Dead!" and begins to decay, rotting seven months in an instant. The tale is gruesome, but the point is clear: will takes precedence over being, decision over time and repetition.

55

The daydream, purgatorial moment between night and day. It is less a source of creativity than a space for creativity, a space for thinking with utter freedom.

56

Sleepwalking and daydreaming, the wandering mind and the wandering body.

57

Dante's jet lag. The poet arrives on the shores at the base of Mount Purgatory early in the morning, after a day's travel. In Jerusalem, at the opposite end of the globe, it is sunset. It is not clear whether Dante and Virgil slept along the journey. I like to imagine the two poets, standing on the deck of their ship, watching the stars and waiting for the great mountain to appear. When they arrive, they are greeted by Cato the Younger, and proceed through the anterooms of purgatory, among the excommunicate, the indolent, the late repentant, and the negligent rulers. Time is marked here by the prayer of the canonical hours. Dante's first sleep in the purgatorial time zone begins after compline, the night prayer. In Purgatory, no climbing is done at night. And as Dante slept on the grass, he dreamt. In his dream, a gold-feathered eagle snatched him up and flew into the sun, and both eagle and poet were annihilated by light and heat.

58

Dante's first night in Purgatory is a portrait of what is in-between: between places, between times, between days, there is a dream that traverses in one swoop the entire trajectory of the purgatorial space. Tellingly, the night-vision that conquers the in-betweens dissipates with the sun's light—its end is also a destruction, a disappearing into the day, a forgetting. This dream is therefore self-effacing, self-forgetting. We are no longer in the liminal here, on the borderlands of different kinds of experience, but within an experience in its own right, a fleeting, transitory moment that brings together the extremes of a concept: infinite and finite, transcendent and immanent, passive and active. For Platonists of all stripes, this is the *metaxu*, the philosopher coming out of himself through speech, communing with ideas by making them present to others. What is in-between, then, is always a kind of ecstasy: I speak, and words go out of me, and they build worlds. But words are always heard. It is up to the hearer to interpret; my word-world is barren until inhabited by the meaning of others—it flies into the sun, just as the dream flies into dawn.

59

J***, his mind addled by benzodiazepines and his common sense by years of psychoanalysis, recounts the crisis that first brought him to the analyst's couch. He was twenty-five and writing a thesis on Spinoza. His days were a series of processions between his rented room in a Parisian attic and the National Library. Because his attic was drafty and stunk of mildew, he would stay in the library until very late. On the night of his breakdown, his lamp was the last one lit in the reading room. Inspired, he wrote with intensity. Page after page came out, as if some demon had possessed him. His tired eyes began to go out of focus. Determined, he would blink and keep writing. Then, in an instant, he was no longer able to read. He recognized the letters on the page, and could name all twenty-six of them. But he had lost the capacity to arrange them into words. What he had just written danced on the page in hieroglyphic mystery. Convinced that it was merely fatigue, J*** packed his things into his briefcase and went home to his attic. In the morning he would read again, he told himself. He collapsed onto his bed and slept profoundly. The next day, nothing had changed. He still found himself in a world of hieroglyphs. That day and those that followed were spent making frantic doctors' visits, going from hospital to hospital and appointment to appoint, explaining to amused physicians that he couldn't read. This tour through the byzantine world of medicine, this cruel burlesque, lasted two weeks. It was then that he had his first appointment the famous analyst JB. J*** lay on the divan and explained his predicament. Then JB stood, went to his bookshelf, and asked if J*** had ever read *Justine*. He gave the open book to his new patient and told him to read the page before him, out loud. Of course, J*** protested. But the extraordinary result was that he was able to proclaim the words on the page without recognizing them as such. He could read out loud even if he couldn't read. J***'s sessions consisted entirely of these recitations until, a few weeks later, having gotten to the terrible confrontation of Justine and the judge, he was able to recognize the words that he spoke.

60

But is the story true? This is the question that plagues those who speak in parables. The storyteller is then obliged to riposte the most irritating of counter questions: *what does it mean for a story to be true?* And because of this, the listener comes to think that all stories have a deeper meaning that the careful interpreter will find. The listener of stories thus becomes an archaeologist of meaning who ultimately brushes away the sand of the story to find the hard fossil of meaning buried underneath. But are the story and its meaning so easily separated? Am I throwing sand in your eyes when I tell you tales? Perhaps this meaning can only be buried in *this* landscape—that is, in *this* story. Brush away a different kind of sediment, and you will find a different meaning.

61

"I don't let my work define me," said N***, nonchalantly. An American diplomat, she was a fine conversationalist, versed in the art of eliciting everything and revealing nothing. But we were in the midst of drinks in a city far away from her assignment, not negotiations. She was right, of course, not to let her work define her. But I could not help but think that the negation was up to mischief. For ultimately *nothing* defines any of us; our mystery belongs to the night, and no accretion of labels can succeed in offering an adequate definition. To be a person means to carry around in oneself a remainder, a contained shadow that resists all cooperation with concepts. The art of living is perhaps more about letting this remainder *be* than rejecting this or that definition of oneself. In tarrying too long with the negative, N*** had implied that some other definition, or a few, plastered one top of another like small bits of gauze on a large wound, would suffice. Personality is not a wound: it is a mystery.

62

I write on little scraps of paper, and their disjointed paragraphs and fragmented phrases litter my desk, where mountains of words amass. To write is to entwine these bits of words and thoughts, so many obstacles to the formation of a story.

63

Nietzsche, writer of night books. One sees him bent over the well-lit table in his rented room in Turin, sorting through pages and notebooks after the landlady's children have gone to sleep. The rattling streetcars, the yelling vendors, and the operetta tunes of the music hall have all yielded to the uniformity of quiet. He is no reader of day books. Of those written in his native tongue, the only one he enjoys is Eckermann's *Conversations with Goethe,* a fragmented book about a picaresque life. His own writing is even more radically fragmented. In daylight, seen by stronger eyes, the papers that he shuffles around on his desk are hopelessly eclectic—or worse, the ravings of a madman. But in the chiaroscuro of candlelight, something special happens, and the madness reveals its wisdom.

64

Philosophers do not like to stay in bed. They place being above nothing, and activity above passivity. One of the most extraordinary ideas of Levinas, in *Time and the Other*, is to celebrate the passivity of sleeping. In doing so, he goes a step further in overcoming the tyranny of the subjective: *I sleep* moves from *I exist* to *it exists*. But what is this "it"? *It* exists can only mean *something exists* in me. And this is night itself: the playground of thinking and being.

65

Insomniacs, too, are keeping vigil in their own way. But the medical tradition—from the medieval up until our own day—is sceptical of this restless watch. *The Anatomy of Melancholy*, in accord with wisdom both ancient and modern, recommends that the insomniac get out of bed and do something else for a while, lest he be overtaken by idle thoughts and never fall asleep. The author of the *Anatomy* does not seem to understand that the insomniac has no energy for crafting idle thoughts. What comes to him are solid things from elsewhere, images with contours and shapes. To let them be and welcome them is an initiation into night-thinking, though of the most tiring sort.

66

Voluptuaries of Sleep III. Paris. H***, who I have known forever, said to me, "I will never marry again. Do you know the reason? I like sleep better than sex. The thought of sharing a bed repulses me. Rolling around in my king-sized bed from dusk until dawn, reading, listening to music, staring at the trees out the window, drifting slowly into sensual dreams—this is my greatest pleasure now." We were sitting in that old café on the rue du Cherche-Midi where we met whenever we both happened to be in town. The infrequency of those meetings meant that our impressions of each other were measured historically: marriages, births, deaths, changes of city or country. I remember H*** when he was a degenerate expat, before the marriage in question. In those days, he spent his endless nights at parties. Now, he was extolling the sleep of celibacy, a sleep, he said, that was accompanied by erotic dreams so vivid that they were more exciting than what his sex life had been. He was on a quest to find the best bed in Paris, a hedonistic pursuit that had consumed his savings. More expensive than prostitutes, he said as he finished the drink he hoped would be his nightcap.

67

Stories, Theories, Prophecies. All our books and speeches belong to one of these three. They are the three ecstasies of words. Stories are told in the past tense, theories expounded in the present, and prophets, preachers, soothsayers, and visionaries speak of the future. The daytime thinker would collapse all three into theory. He does not realize that his own mode of speech is an ecstasy, too.

68

A word is the product of a will. But once I have spoken, the will that produced it retreats, and the word continues to move forward. Once thoughts have been given velocity, they don't need the thinker anymore.

69

R*** told the following story: "During a certain period of my life, I made frequent visits to Prague. Even if these visits were only ever very short, I felt as if the city had become a part of me, and exerted an inexplicable hold on me. Whenever I arrived, my feet would carry me along the cobblestone all by themselves, as if the map of Prague were lodged deep in my body. I would never think about where I was going, because I knew that thinking would only mislead me. One of these experiences proved to be particularly intense. I got off the plane, left my luggage at the seedy hotel in the Lower Town where I always stayed, and went out into the street. My legs began to propel me forward. As if possessed by a demon, I walked. The sun was setting, the taverns were full, and the streets were busy. I walked up to the castle, down again across the Charles Bridge, through the old town, past the factories of the Karlin District, and up towards Letna Park. In the working-class neighborhood east of the Park, I went up and down streets and across boulevards, looking for something that I could not name. I inspected the houses, with their lights on and their owners moving about the rooms. Then I came to a halt, stopping in front of one house in particular. I stood there for a long time before I went up to ring the bell. It was a house that looked like all the others. A man about my height and build opened the door. He had not turned on the hallway light, and I could not make out his features in the dark. He asked me what

I wanted. I told him who I was, and that I had come to visit. The man answered that he had known a man of my profession from my country a long time ago, but that he had lost contact with this acquaintance years before. In any case, he had no desire to entertain at this hour. He closed the door, and I went back into street. I was completely lost. The desire to walk had left me. I had not eaten since I had arrived. I summoned up all my remaining strength and began to walk. But I was hopelessly lost. Nothing looked familiar; I knew none of the street names and recognized none of the buildings. It was night and the city was empty. Around four in the morning, I wandered into Wenceslas Square and found a taxi that took me back to my hotel. The next day, I tried to remember where I had been. I had likely wandered into the sixth district north of the park, and from there to Wenceslas Square should have been at most a forty-minute walk, through familiar streets. But I had been utterly lost. And in the clarity of daylight, I was unsure of where the house had been. I decided not to look for it.

70

The wanderer, even if an essentially urban figure, flitting from square to square and bench to bench, is not welcome in the modern city. If he was once able to savor the city in the open (Baudelaire), his playground is soon closed in by arcades, storefronts, automobiles, deliveries, spectacles (Benjamin). It is only when the stores close and the money changers have gone to bed that the *flaneur* is really free.

71

For as long as we have been creating images, we have been destroying them—and indeed, perhaps the destructive, iconoclastic impulse is older than the artistic one. In antiquity, art and religion are inseparable. And how could a human face, suddenly, miraculously emerging from stone, not be the appearance of a god? No matter about the artist (in any case, there were no artists in those days, only craftsmen): the image made itself. And so the work of art appears to be the odyssey of Truth outside of itself, lost in the world of representation. It would seem that it is the concept of representation that makes the destruction of images possible; the image is an inadequate representation of a reality so fundamental that its false depiction is dangerous. Some time around 730, Emperor Leo III ordered that the image of Christ be removed from above the Chalke Gate, the entrance to the Byzantine palace of Constantinople. The volcano of Santorini had erupted, many had died, and the Emperor took this to be a sign of God's punishment; like the Israelites in the desert, his people had forged idols to worship, and earned God's wrath. For a generation, the Empire would be divided into iconodules, who saw images of God as a pathway to the divine, and iconoclasts, for whom these representations were seducers, imprisoning the soul in the material world of lies and deception. Icons and frescos were defaced, men were killed, the icon painters fled. For the iconoclast theologian, there are no adequate representations of God other than his being made present again in the fullness of his divinity—in the host during the Divine Liturgy. A eucharistic Church has no icons. Interestingly, no iconodule would have objected to Constantine's destruction, after his conversion, of images of the old gods. These representations, then, are not inadequate (as the iconoclasts say of pious representations of the Christian god) but too adequate. Given this reversal, we could perhaps reverse the question behind the debate about images: can the creation of an image itself be an iconoclastic act? One cannot help but wonder whether the Italian renaissance, which restores the images of the old gods destroyed by Constantine, is not a kind of destruction of destruction. This idea becomes clearer when art moves into the abstract. Surrealism and cubism, Picasso, Miró, and Klee—are not seeking adequate representations, but undermining the very idea of representation. This sentiment can be pushed into nihilist extremes. In the ugly, shocking, and absurd works of some contemporary artists, the image has become a self-erasing artifice, leaving only the idea behind. They succeed in producing a primordial uncanniness—the feeling that iconoclasm is what makes art possible.

72

The Germans are nature lovers, and their thinkers are no different. There are forest-thinkers (Heidegger) and mountain-thinkers (Nietzsche), but where are the river-thinkers? I am a city creature, but if forced to think in open air, I would be a *Bächleindenker*, hopping from rock to rock, watching the stream of water part around my footsteps.

73

Perchance to dream IV. The *Hypnerotomachia Poliphili,* a work by an anonymous author, was printed in Venice in 1499. While there is no author indicated on the title page, an acrostic can be formed from the first letter of every chapter that spells out the name of Francesco Colonna, poet and preacher at St Mark's Cathedral. The book is an *incunable,* or product of the earliest days of the printing press (the first Gutenberg Bible is from 1452), and dazzles with its magnificent woodcut illustrations. It leads us through an oneiric Quattrocento courtly love affair, surreal and comical, written in a peculiar latinized Italian sprinkled with Greek words and bogus hieroglyphs. Our hero, Poliphilio (the "many-friended") wanders through an arcadian dreamland in search of his lost beloved, Polia ("many things"). The woodcuts render the dreamscape more convincingly than the story does: Poliphilio wanders through forests peopled with dragons, is kidnapped by nymphs, sails to a Greek island on a boat captained by Cupid, and united with his beloved by Venus. These scenes are separated by a series of narcoleptic swoons in which Poliphilio suddenly falls asleep, being transported into another dreamscape. This Russian doll construction of dreams-within-dreams is broken by the incursion of Polia's narrative voice, with the beloved complaining in not-so-romantic tones about Poliphilo's delusional conviction that *she* is the one who is in love with him—he thinks, in spite of his pursuit, that he is the beloved, not the lover. His delusional triumph is short. When the lovers, reunited by the goddess, finally kiss, Polia instantly vanishes, and Poliphilio wakes up from his infinite regress of dreams. In spite of its numerous illustrations, this madcap story—perhaps the first genuinely baroque work of art—is impossible to follow. Indeed, to really understand its movements, one must walk through the Garden of Bomarzo, some sixty-eight kilometers north of Rome. Colloquially known as the Park of Monsters, its Orcus mouth, Cerberus, Hannibal's elephant, leaning house, and temple are a stone version of the *Hypnerotomachia*. Under the beautiful Italian sun, one passes from dream to dream, and never wakes up.

74

The Future. Is it the dawn, or something else, something that does not leave the night?

75

I remember thee upon my bed III. In those days, the word of the Lord was rare. Or was it? Perhaps he spoke too softly, at times when most were asleep. Samuel, assistant to the priest Eli, lay in his bed. In the night, The Lord whispered his name, *Samuel, Samuel.* The boy rose and went to Eli. You called me, he said, and I have come. But no one had called him, and Eli sent him back to bed. Again, Samuel heard his name, and again, he went to Eli. And Eli sent him back to bed. For a third time, Samuel heard his name, and went to Eli. The old priest now understood. He told the boy, if you hear the call again, stay in your bed, and say, speak Lord, your servant is listening! And so it came to pass that when Samuel heard his name, he said, speak Lord, your servant is listening! And the Lord spoke to him. What was said is as unimportant as who called and who heard: no one seemed to have called Samuel, and since he went three times to Eli rather than stay in his bed, no one was listening. Samuel's spiritual task was to forget who was calling and who was listening, to forget any content, to abandon all goals. It was in pure passivity, in simply receiving, that Samuel became the Servant of the Lord. *And so he lay down until morning.*

76

I will tell your future: it is contained in the choice you have already made. Look back to your oldest decision, and there is your future.

77

A young Dane named Søren goes to Berlin to study. He leaves Copenhagen by train at a certain time, and rides a certain coach into the city, sitting in a certain place. He takes a certain cab at a certain street corner to a certain house, where he rented a room. The landlord, the manservant, the university, the old professor, the river, the Gendarmenmarkt, the streets with their linden trees all make a certain impression. Some years later in Copenhagen, Søren is in crisis. He calls off a marriage engagement, packs his trunk, and leaves for Berlin. He takes that same certain train at the same certain time as before; he sits in the same coach, takes a cab at the same certain street corner; he rents the same room in the same certain building, where the same manservant opens up the same old trunk. At the university, the same old professor is talking about the same old things; the Gendarmenmarkt, the river, and the linden trees are exactly as they were. And yet this perfect repetition of the past could not bring him back to the days before his crisis, and the decisions they provoked. Worse still, this whole mass of certain things brought him no certainty. He was condemned to keep on deciding.

78

Gentle reader! I am not an astrophysicist, and no great philosopher either. I cannot tell you what Time is. Besides, this little book is not about such lofty daytime topics—one needs a well-lit room to read about those things. In the starless night, one can only talk about the *experience* of time; not of the time that we live in, but the time that lives in us. Only those who have sat in the dark know that we feel within us a deep before and a deep after, those times that are unreachable. In the felt infinity of night, the previous day belongs to another age, as does the day to come.

79

In Auerbach's cellar. Doctor Faustus makes a deal with the devil. The wager—at least as Goethe tells the story—is that the devil will never be able to present Faust with an experience that captivates him, and that he would not want to end. The devil Mephistopheles begins by trying the simplest of solutions. He brings Faust to a tavern, where those for whom every day is a holiday drink and sing until dawn. The old devil himself joins in on the fun, and tells a story about an emperor who befriends a flee. Faust is bored. He would rather be in bed. It is strange how easily Faust is able to transform night passion into daytime seriousness. The night reveller stays in the same place, he sings, he does not notice the passage of time, soon the tavern is closing, he must go, drinking one last glass of beer hastily, standing near the door. The person obliged by daytime law to stay in the same place, no matter how comfortable, is insufferably bored, and would rather be anywhere else than that place of duty, where time drags on. This acedia, this noonday devil, is Faust's malady. Through the sheer force of his Apollonian will, he feels it even at midnight.

80

Perchance to dream V. Animals dream, but do they act in the day based on their dreams? What sort of beast, then, gives prophetic weight to its night visions? Only *homo ludens*. We do not write down our dreams to determine their meaning, or even to bestow meaning on them. We write them down because *it is a game*. Or better yet: writing down our dreams is one of the variants of our favorite game, meaning making and meaning divining. Like all games, its rules have become more elaborate with time. When the old philosophers first began to play this game, they would merely point at things and ask "what is that?" They found this boring activity suspiciously amusing. The source of this amusement is a doubling that takes place in the *doxa*, or the opining about what something seems to be. Language does not seem to grasp immediately what things are, but compares its ideas about something with the way it appears. To ask "what is that?" is to make something present as a "what" that is something (*to ti esti*), or to use Aristotle's more elegant expression, the "what" that I reckon "that" has become (*to ti en einai*). The very form of these questions doubles the object into "what" and "that", and the game is to make them correspond. The old Greek rulebook of this game limits the solutions to a *doxa*: I make statements about the way things seem to be. But we must amend these rules to talk about dreams, since the dream has no *doxa* until it has been written down. The writing of the dream yields the "what [it] has become." The dream exploits the paradox at the heart of all *doxa*: that things *seem* to be this way or that way is already an achievement, already the product of some prior meaning-making. How, then, do we play that game of dream interpretation? We posit the dream and its meaning together in language, *as if* they were part of a complete, enclosed system: dreams are truly expressed in language and say something (*dokein*) about the meaning of my world. But the dream is, by definition, that which resists systematicity. The dream is a *promissory note* (*symbolon*), a ticket that lets you play the game of meaning-making. Tell your dream, and you have bought your ticket to the meaning games. Play, enjoy yourself, and don't worry too much about the validity of the things you say. More important is your absorption in the game. When you emerge, you will have developed a handy skill for dealing with *doxa* and its paradoxes: symbolic thinking.

81

In Sarajevo, a talentless old singer, toothless and breathless, his lute missing strings, wanders up and down the market street from the wooden fountain to the mosque by the river. He only knows one song, and he sings it badly.

82

Melancholia IV. Saturn, at once distant star and ancient god, is the sign under which the melancholic lives. Saturn-Kronos, son of Ouranos, the sky, is the greatest of the Titans, and presides over a golden age that precedes the strife of Olympian reign. Knowing that his children posed a threat to his kingdom, he devoured them all when they were born. Only Zeus, born in secret, survives to maturity, and can vanquish his father. Kronos is god of the Past. For who remembers a time before the mighty Zeus reigned on Olympus? Who is older than the king of the gods? Certainly, no mortal. Only the earth and the sky remember the days of Kronos, who was already old when time began, and who is so averse to the future that he devoured his own possibilities. Once overthrown by Zeus, the old man is hurled into the lowest part of the heavens, the *imum caeli,* at the very foundations of the universe. Saturn, far from the sun's warmth, is a cold and windy planet. It radiates with the dual energy of the wise old man who is also destructive ogre. When it is visible in the sky, a spirit of indolence reigns; dropsy and rheumatism, the diseases of the old man, spread; even sanguine souls are possessed by bitterness, despondency, and pettiness. Those given to overmuch study are by their profession given over to Saturn, who is able to drive them into creative frenzy. Saturn, for the ancients the farthest planet from us, exerts nonetheless the most powerful influence on the affairs of earth. Those under its influences are people of extremes, *perittoi*: "in one and the same person, the most excellent and most unfortunate, like Herakles; the wisest and most ignorant, like Socrates; the most blasphemous and holiest, like Empedocles."

83

We have already spoken of night books and day books. But does the act of writing itself belong to the night? I do not mean Proust lying in bed with pen and notebooks, or Balzac working furiously until dawn. What I mean is writing as the sustained creation of a space in which a work can emerge of its own accord. Creating this space requires a kind of self-effacement, since if the self does not withdraw, if it does not become an empty container for the work, no writing can happen. Great men do not write books, because their "I" saturates their creative endeavours. As Blanchot says, it is when we can pass from *I* to *he* or *she* that writing begins. Why else do so many writers keep notebooks and journals? To gather material, you say. On the contrary, writers' diaries exist to a preserve a self that is otherwise only a scaffolding.

84

Why do we sleep? I have asked the question to every scientist willing to listen. It is inevitably met with confusion. They usually misunderstand it as, why do we *need* to sleep? and talk about hormonal balance, cellular regeneration, and neuronal connection. But that was not the question: why do we sleep? Why, when the sun sets, do our spirits start to fade, and consciousness disappears until the light returns? Why do I spend one third of my existence—if not more!—in a state that mirrors non-existence? But this is perhaps the wrong way of addressing the bivalence of sleeping and waking. What if, rather than a loss of existence, sleep were instead a refuge from the hegemony of being? And not sleeping would be, rather than consciousness regained, the drying up of being's wellspring, an affront to the activities of the day rather than the obscurity of the night. Insomnia, that vigil in which we can only accept the opaque things that present themselves to us, is a moment that suspends subjectivity even more than sleep: it is a nonsubjective event, pure presence, a suspension of the rhythm of existence, an interruption of Being's act: like Penelope, each night it unmakes what it made during the day: itself.

85

The masked philosopher, hiding behind the cypher of language, speaks in many ways, adopting many roles. Each person in a dialogue—even the wise Socrates—tells lies, and none of them adequately express the truth the philosopher wants to convey. The problem, of course, is the very representation of truth: there is always a distance between the idea and its representation, an ironic gap that cannot be bridged. The philosopher, then, can only conjure up a series of images, all of which gesture toward the Idea from different positions. But if the philosopher is focused on the ineffability of what is utterly true, the poet is concerned with the irreducibility of representations to an idea—try to reduce literature to allegory, and there will always be a piece that does not fit. Hence the allegorical-interpretive approach of the philosopher and the ironic-creative approach of the poet are opposite directions along the same path, one that never quite reaches the destination that it sets for itself.

86

M***, a student at Oxford, says that she often wakes up in the middle of the night, wondering if she will live to be forty. Pale, thin, and dressed in black, she is writing a thesis on medieval philosophy and radiates a spirit of ascetism. She is strong-willed and in excellent health. But at night, the fragility of the first half of life, the tenuous existence of the young person, not yet who she ought to be, seems unbearable. If M*** is still worried about the tenuousness of life, I have crossed the border into that worry of the second half of life: its finitude.

87

E***, who I knew as a student of history in Tübingen, returned to his native Zurich after his studies and slowly amassed one of the largest private libraries in Switzerland. Already when we were at university, he had been an incorrigible bibliomaniac. More than once, I accompanied him to Stuttgart on the earliest train, with both of us carrying our empty suitcases. We would return to Tübingen in the evening with E***'s purchases, carrying them up the five flights of stairs to his spacious attic room. When asked if he had read them all, E*** would simply roll his eyes. Later, in Zurich, E*** had access to both world-class book dealers and a nearly bottomless inheritance. This fuelled his passion for books from the earliest days of the printing press: renaissance prayer books bound in vellum; illustrated copies of the mystical treatises of Jakob Boehme; ancient prints of Ficino's Plato translations; and a copy of Nicholas of Cusa's *De docta ignorantia* from the beginning of the sixteenth century. As both his expertise and his appetite grew, E*** had ever more frequent recourse to the black market. All of the items in the temperature-controlled room at the back of his flat belonged in museums. Some had been forcibly taken from them. E***'s passion soon descended into obsession. Happily, I was not there to witness its unfurling, and what I now relate was communicated to me by a mutual acquaintance. E*** was on the hunt for the most difficult of acquisitions imaginable: a Gutenberg Bible. Of the 150 or 180 to have been printed, 49 are known to have survived. Of these, only 21 are complete, with the others having lost pages. E***, however, was convinced that there was at least one more complete copy, and that it was owned by a Saudi prince. His days were spent making frantic enquiries. In the evening, he would return to sit in his great library, examining his collection with a mixture of pleasure and disgust—the cornerstone, the crowning jewel, the Gutenberg Bible, was missing. It was during one of these evenings that E*** heard a murmur coming from the bookshelves. A faint lament, a complaint like the distant barking of a seal. He searched the entire library until he found its source: it was coming from behind a first-edition copy of *Little Dorrit*. He removed the book, and saw nothing. It was only once he opened the book that the sound stopped. It was as if it were crying to be read. He replaced it, drank a glass of schnapps, and went to bed. From the bedroom, the seal-like complaint of books could be heard. They grew louder and louder. E*** sprang out of bed and began the laborious task of finding the books that were crying, and opening them. He ran from one end of the book-lined apartment to the other in a frenzy, opening and closing books. Soon it seemed that the whole library was wailing, and he began to throw the open books on the floor. This proved to be only a temporary solution. By dawn, the books lamented open-mouthed, their deafening cries bringing E*** to the edge of despair. There was only one thing to do: he opened the living-room windows wide, and began to throw books into the street. Armful after armful flew onto the pavement. The Neugasse was soon barricaded by a whirlwind of paper, and the pages blew into the Langstrasse, causing at least two traffic accidents. By the time the police arrived, more than ten thousand books had been thrown into the street, and E***, exhausted, lay sobbing on the floor. Fortuitously, the rare books in their temperature-controlled room were separated from the rest of the collection by a thick metal door, and their cries had not been heard. When our mutual acquaintance visited E*** at the alpine clinic where he will no doubt finish his unhappy life, he said that he longed to see his rare books more than anything. The clinic was not so bad, he said, but the bare walls filled him with sadness.

88

How easy to lose one's sense of self in the dark! As I go about my daytime occupations, the repetitions and uniforms of the self continually reinforce my identity. There are, however, incursions of darkness into this clarity about myself: I can dissociate from who I am, retreat into some dark corner of my personality, or even assume the character of some other within me. The speculative range of dissociation is vast, from daydreams and feelings of uncanniness, to dissonant dissociative fugues all the way to the complete loss of personality. These strongest instances, of course, are pathological, a sinking of self into obscurity. Yet its opposite is not mindfulness but solipsism, which is nothingness—even if in daylight, it presents itself as a grand fortress to be explored. At night, one cannot see the distant countryside, and the strong battlements and drawn bridges are transformed from a guarantee of safety to a form of oppression. Personality is always a kind of separation from oneself, the going beyond oneself that is the movement of life. A little dissociation (but no more than that!) is necessary: it is the inexplicable foundation of our personality, the night in us.

89

Melancholia V. Saturnalia and Revolution. During the Roman festival of Saturnalia, all of society is turned upside down: gambling is legal, masters become servants, and a fool is emperor for a day. This not only removes pressure from a rigid society; it lets the opposites exist alongside each other. The festival is curative. Today, there are no festivals, and all social powers are hegemonic. Saturn reigns as despot until he is overthrown. The inability to sustain opposites therefore yields to violence. Where chaos is outlawed, order disintegrates.

90

Perchance to dream VI. M.N., a neurotic writer, was anxious about a dream, and insisted on telling it to me. It took place in a castle on a narrow isthmus, which on closer inspection proved to be a kind of naval garrison. He was standing in a large dining hall with the commander of the fort. By the tall windows that looked out onto the sea were large buttresses and a complex system of fortifications. The dreamer understood that he was a volunteer naval officer, and the commander, who was about to leave, was instructing him on what to do when the enemy attacked. Above all, the Great Hall would have to be evacuated in order to protect the civilians—the commander's family was living in the fort, and his wife was ill. The dreamer asked him how they should communicate in case of emergency, but the commander had no time to answer—he fell to the floor, dead. The dreamer then went to one of the tall windows. A steady stream of merchant ships sailed past. Suddenly, his brother appeared at his side, and said to him, *look at this ship over there? Is it friendly?* M.N. awoke before he saw the ship his brother had pointed out. "The dream itself wasn't frightening," he told me, "but there was something uncanny about it, something I don't understand. It sounds strange, but I have the feeling that this dream has been dreamt before. Not by me, it was entirely new to me, but by someone else. It's as if this were *someone else's dream.*"—"Of course it is," I answered. "And the ship that you did not see is indeed friendly. It was the breakfast ship." M.N. grew very pale, and instead of returning to the library, went home to lie down.

91

The eponymous protagonist of Borges's *Pierre Menard, Author of the Quixote* (1939) is a great French literary scholar from Nîmes who approaches *Don Quixote* in the most impossible of ways. He wants neither to write a book about Cervantes, nor to translate his masterwork. And so he sought to create an exact reproduction of it, in his own words—except that those words happen to be exactly those of the original: "Pierre Menard did not want to compose *another* Quixote, which surely is easy enough—he wanted to compose *the* Quixote." He did not want to copy it, but instead "produce a number of pages which coincided—word for word and line for line—with those of Miguel de Cervantes." Our critic-narrator, presenting his own literary opuscule within the bounds of Borges's story in such a way that one wonders if he is not a double of Pierre Menard just as Menard's book is a double of Cervantes's, tells us that this second version is *better* than the original. Key to this ironic affirmation is the fact that Menard did not reproduce the whole book, but only chapters nine, thirty-eight, and part of twenty-two from the first part. There is therefore a quixotic remainder, such that when one reads chapter sixteen (as our narrator does), one finds in Cervantes a style vaguely reminiscent of Menard, but certainly more primitive, not nearly as good as Menard's chapter thirty-eight, with its allusive Nietzscheanism and intertextual flair. Between same and same, the quixotic remainder makes all the difference.

In *The Circular Ruins* (1940), Borges pushes this idea even further. After arriving at the ruins of an ancient temple, a man spends a year going about an impossible task: dreaming another man into existence. Overcoming both problems of method and bouts of insomnia, the dreamer constructs a man piece by piece, until this dream phantasm is human down to the smallest detail. The problem, of course, is how to confer existence on this dream-being. A fire god then appears to him in a dream and promises to externalize his creation. Only the dreamer and the god would know that the dream-man is really an illusion. The dreamer then spends a year educating his dream-Frankenstein before sending him off to another ruined temple nearby. But before he does so, he erases his creature's memory of his apprenticeship, lest he know that he is only a dream. When both temples are subject to forest fires, he realizes that neither of them can be harmed by fire. The dreamer therefore realizes that he, too, is only the dream of another, made real by the fire god. Pierre Menard was almost such a dreamer: his initial idea was to *become* Miguel de Cervantes, something that would allow him to reproduce the Quixote out of sheer necessity. This, he thought, was too easy: much more demanding would be to reproduce the Quixote *as Pierre Menard*. Anyone can dream, but only fire gods can perform the ontological argument, giving existence to what one already finds as a complete being. But let me put it less abstractly: Pierre Menard is not only the secret narrator of his own story, he is the quixotic author of *The Circular Ruins*, albeit from within the confines of his own story. My textual proof is the strange footnote that closes the text of *Pierre Menard*: "I recall his square-ruled notebooks, his black crossings-out, his peculiar typographical symbols, and his insect-like handwriting. In the evening, he liked to go out for walks on the outskirts of Nîmes; he would often carry along a notebook and make a cheery bonfire."

92

Levinas thinks that the night is characterized by *horror*. But he is a man of hyperboles, a night-writer who dresses thoughts in phantasmagoria. His point is that when one is faced with the idea of nothing, one feels angst, but when faced with the idea of an unidentifiable *something*, one feels horror. This is the uncanny in another key, like when one arrives in an unknown city after a long journey. The city moves and breathes, its heart beats. Then I am thrown into it. I have no place there, no function, nothing to do. There is no passage here from "it is" to "I am." If lying on one's deathbed is the opposite movement—the world once again becomes merely *it is*, monolithic and other, as *I am* retreats into oblivion—then being thrown into an *it is* to which I do not belong makes me see things through their crepuscule. This experience of horror is a moment of night in broad daylight, a loneliness that only comes in the dark.

93

Eternal Return. Perhaps you already know this haunting story: A demon comes to you in the night, in your loneliest hour, and tells you that the life you have lived, every moment, every detail, will be repeated an infinite number of times. Do you curse the demon, or do you fall on your knees and call him a god? The demon sees, but does not understand. For *before* he came, I had already chosen my life—before the sequence of eternal lives, I chose what I would be. All that I learn from this divine messenger is that my decision stands above the temporal sequence of the everyday.

94

Nicodemus goes to Jesus at night, in secret. During the day, the Jesus of John's Gospel performs signs. In the night, he speaks secret wisdom, sphinx-like. Unless you are born again of water and wind, you will have no life in you. How can one be born again if one has already left the mother's womb? The night itself is the Johannine womb, and John's Church is the Church that has not yet dawned, the Church of those who tell secrets at night.

95

I fell into the arms of Morpheus, the French say. They mean, quite simply, *I fell asleep,* and quickly. Morpheus—and perhaps this is why the French have adopted him—is more literary than mythological. He is Ovid's invention. One of the thousand sons of Somnus, god and personification of Sleep, Morpheus's name indicates his vocation: *morphe* means form, and the *somnia* are faces that people our dreams. Morpheus is the artificer, the artisan whose work is his own appearance. In the *Metamorphoses,* Iris, the messenger goddess, comes to Morpheus to relay a message from Juno (Hera) to Alcyone. Morpheus must send Alycone a nightmare announcing the death at sea of her beloved, Ceyx. His portrait of a Ceyx beyond the grave is so convincing that, upon waking, Alycone rushes to the shore, where the body of Ceyx has come in on the tide. As she embraces the corpse, both are turned into Kingfisher—the meaning of Alcyone's name in Greek. Morpheus plays only a minor role in all this, a bit part, but one that distracted so well that he is better remembered than Alcyone. This is all the more remarkable when we recall that Morpheus's very name implies he has no content, only form. To fall into his arms is to fall into a world of possibilities, to enter into a den of shapeshifters and tragicomedians, shuffling on and off stage in ever-changing costumes. Morpheus holds us in his arms, our dreams contain us. Their unknown content must lay somewhere outside the realm of sleep.

96

Having escaped the baroque decay of Sicily that he hated so passionately, the ever-restless P*** made his way to Oslo, where he accepted a temporary position at the university. After weeks without news, I received a message: "The Nordic sky reminds me that we have been meaning to talk about Rilke for a long time, but never did. Would you agree that Rilke and Proust represent two opposite directions in which twentieth century literature simultaneously moves? If Proust opens his *Recherche* with waking up and continues with an investigation into how we affirm life, so Rilke starts his *Aufzeichnungen* with falling asleep, and continues with an exposition of how much death and the dead populate our lives."

The Book *of* Nocturnes

97

Pillow talk. A thousand years ago, a Persian Shah discovered that his wife had committed adultery. He had her beheaded. Afterwards, he married a virgin every day, and had her beheaded the next morning so that she could not betray him. Soon his viziers could find no more virgins. Only one remained in the whole Empire: the crafty Scheherazade. After they had made love, Scheherazade began to tell the Shah a story. He was so captivated that he lost track of time. Then, just as the story was reaching its climax, Scheherazade stopped. It is dawn, she said, and I must go to my beheading. But the Shah, wanting to hear the rest of the story, stayed her execution, and told her to resume the next night. After they had made love, Scheherazade finished the story. It was the middle of the night, and the Shah wanted to hear another. But just as the night before, Scheherazade came to the best part of her story as dawn broke. The Shah again stayed her execution, and told her to return at dusk. This continued for a thousand and one nights. After a thousand stories, Scheherazade announced that there was nothing left to tell, and she asked to say goodbye to the three sons to whom she had given birth since she had been made consort. But the Shah had fallen in love with Scheherazade, and that day, he crowned her Shah-Zan, Queen of Persia. This old story contains a thousand stories whose content remains unknown to us. Even if the excitement that these stories produce in the Shah is the lynchpin of the tale, it is achieved without any reference to content. This story, then, is a story about the telling and not the told, a play of pure form. And just as we do not know, from our daytime perch, what stories were told, the Shah, upon waking from his morning slumber, may not even have remembered what he had been told. All that is necessary for the plot (and the plots-within-the-plot) to progress is the desire to be absorbed in a narrative outside of which nothing is visible. Meanwhile, the day runs its course, sons are born, and we turn the pages of *One Thousand and One Nights.* The nocturnal imperceptibly transforms the diurnal, form mirrors form in the dark, just as object mirrors object in the light. Then, on the dawn of the day after the play of forms has exhausted itself, something new emerges.

98

Where I am, it is still night, I cannot sleep, and I have no Shah-Zan of my own to tell me stories until dawn, so I will dwell for a little longer with Scheherazade. She is also a philosophy, you know. Or perhaps I should say, she *is* philosophy, she reveals the mytho-poetic origins of philosophy. Before Plato and Socrates separated themselves from the poets, the madness of poetry was considered to be inextricably bound to the reason of scientific inquiry— that is, philosophy. The very word, the love of wisdom, lends itself to poetic excess. Like troubadours, many of the pre-Socratics and Sanskrit sages explained the world in verse. And to this day, those unfamiliar with the theories of the physicists and biologists read the great poem of nature, as people have always done. The stories and songs of ancient peoples pass on wisdom about how one lives, and provide instructions for that most delicate exercise: emerging from the wild. There is an aesthetic continuity in the history of science that forms a poetic popular science, a poetic life-wisdom that says in images what the scholar will say in argument. But there are limits to this way of thinking. If we say, for example, that all knowledge is aesthetic, we will go looking for the arguments within the stories, or worse, telling stories that are not stories at all, but veiled arguments. Moreover, we will then want to go looking for the pre-conditions for theory that lurk behind the story, and the poetic will have been entirely obliterated. I prefer a simpler solution: the story is to the night what the theory is to the day. And if the thoughts of the day are never-ending—for thought always turns in on itself—the stories of the night have a beginning and an end. It is precisely as reprieve from the wheel of thought that a Scheherazade story is effective, and can bring about an impossible transmutation of thought: the next day, we are inexplicably different, and even if we can project an explanation onto this after the fact, it does not change what is most important: we could not have achieved the same with our day-thoughts.

99

Melancholia VI. The early modern philosophy of melancholy can be summed up in an elaborate engraving from Albrecht Dürer, *Melencholia* I (1514). It is starkly black and white. A winged female figure sits on a plain bench in jarring contrast to the clutter around her. Her head rests on her closed fist as she stares into the distance gloomily, ignoring everything around her: the compass in her hand; the closed book on her lap; and the bell, hourglass and sundial that hang above her. Her gaze travels out wearily from beneath her crown of watercress, away from the keys and the purse that hang from her belt, away from the miscellany that lies at her feet—the hammer and nails, the plane and pincers, the saw and straightedge, the syringe and the bellows, the inkwell and pen, the brazier and the alchemist's crucible. She ignores the scraggy dog that sleeps at her feet, and the cherub that sits on a chipped millstone, writing, a balance scale hanging above him. Behind her stands a windowless building that is nothing at all, and that nobody visits, seven rungs of an endless ladder propped up against it. She even manages to ignore the most bewitching objects: the perfect sphere in front of her, the hourglass and magic square behind her, the bat that carries the banner that announces the theme: *Melencholia* I. Her gloom is pervasive, it rises above all this, it traverses worlds. Indeed, no work of art has elicited so many books, so many opuscules and treatises, as this sad little *gravure*. Every object here contains its world of symbolism—not only of melancholy, but of mathematics. Indeed, the winged protagonist flies not in body but in mind, and her tools are not only those of an alchemist, but a mathematician. At once Lady Melancholy and Lady Geometry, she is above all a Saturnine Sophia: Saturn's wisdom is sad, his sadness is wisdom.

100

Death Fugue. The polluted water flowed thick in the night under his feet, black milk of the evening passing invisibly as he paced. He had walked up and down the bridge for hours now, down along one side of the railing and then up along the other. Did he have the courage? He could not bear to call it by its name. As he paced in varied rhythms, reciting arguments and old conversations like prayers, there was a mental censure upon that one word, that smallest of words, three letters in his own language—in the language that he had used, anyway. In the same language, an old question was repeated: *Nun sag, wie hast du's mit der Religion?* What are your religious convictions? There were no words for this question either. When he had been in Jerusalem the year before, the Talmud scholars and the readers of the Kabbalah told him that there were no words to bridge the gap between man and God: we cannot say what God is, only what God is not. He had replied: we are not God, and yet we cannot say what we are, either. To this the Talmud scholars had no answer. And so he went to the Master in the Black Forest, picked arnica, and listened as the Master kept silent. We do not have words, the Master wrote, the words have us, and, blue-eyed and lusty, they set their hounds upon us, and captured us, and fed us black milk. His feet were really beginning to hurt now. How long had he been pacing? He had walked around the Shrine of the Book in Jerusalem with the Talmud scholars, and deep into the Black Forest with the Master. The Talmudists would talk, and the Master would keep silent. Ingeborg would tell him what the Master meant; in long letters or sleepless nights, lying in her narrow bed in Vienna, narrow as a grave, she would explain the silence. She had perished in flames after acting out her own ridiculous *auto-da-fé*. Now there were only the loquacious Talmud scholars and the silent Master. How his feet hurt! The river flowed beneath the bridge, its noise and stench overpowering his thoughts. How much water had passed by since he first came here, earlier in the evening? The water swallowed all things up, his thoughts were already submerged in it, the sentences of his inner monologue broken by its sound. No matter: there were no words anyway. The last half-formed thought he had before he passed over the railing was, *how barbaric to write poems when so many of us are gone...*

101

On the night of 23 November 1654, the renowned geometer Blaise Pascal is roused from sleep by a fantastic vision: *Fire, the God of Abraham, Isaac, and Jacob, Certainty, Certainty, Certainty...* The experience lasts for two hours. What was revealed to Pascal was not the God of the philosophers, but of the patriarchs, and of Jesus Christ. The conclusion is radical: *Forget the world and everything in it; there is only God.* The great mathematician, the man who had looked for a Prime Mover and Self-Thinking Thought, was cast out of his intellectual system, propelled beyond the world of lines and curves. He is at pains to describe what happened. In his written account of it, the *Memorial*, he says nothing of what he saw, speaking only of what he experienced. We call this event his "night of fire," but fire would seem to be only one metaphor among others: certainty, the patriarchs, Christ, the folly of worldly life. In this spirit, the *Memorial* is less an account than it is a manifesto, a promise that Pascal hopes to realize, and that so totally describes his life's mission that he has two copies of the text sown into his shirt. Had his fellow geometers read the text, they may well have protested that it is a sort of religious raving, a text that does not say anything. And this, Pascal might answer, is precisely the point: the ineffable God who filled the human heart with boundless desires can only address the heart, and speaks the one boundless Word that is too tremendous for human words to repeat—his own name, his own deepest self.

102

Sometime around 420 AD, Simeon Stylites the Elder climbed up a pillar that was part of a ruined roman temple, and lived a contemplative life atop it for some forty years. The surface area of his pillar top would have been about the size of a monk's cell. Food was sent up in baskets, and the locals gathered at the foot of the pillar, wondering at the holiness of this contemplative whose only temptation was to come down. Simeon was not the first to live like this: adepts of the god Dionysius once climbed to the top of phallic pillars, imploring the god for prosperity. Did Simeon know about this Dionysiac past? He at least knew that his perch was once the buttress of a temple, his spiritual life built on the ruins of the dead religion of a dying empire. Simeon's secret is hidden in plain sight all over Europe: the splendours of Christendom—the mosaics of Byzantium, the Cathedrals of the Loire, the frescos of the Papal States—they are all fed by ruins. Nature itself is built on the ruins of its own past, nourished by the fossils and detritus that achieved their present state after terrible strife. This is the terrible secret of all things present: our origins are really ruins, and harken back to extinctions past.

103

The night is not a place, not the way the day is. It may be empty, but it cannot be peopled with things and objects and presences as can the day. When one seeks to make the day present in the night, one need only fall asleep, and in the oblivion that sleep brings, one prepares oneself for a day of action—in sleeping, we nourish the day. But making night present to the day requires the radical act of refusing to sleep, or not sleeping. The insomniac, his eyes red and puffy, treads across the day like a sleepwalker: he is ineffectual, tired, spent already at the beginning. "People who sleep badly always appear to be guilty of something," writes Maurice Blanchot. "What have they done? They have made the night present to us."

104

Orpheus, son of Apollo, learned to use the lyre that his father gave him. His were the oldest and most beautiful songs of the Greek world, envy of Homer and Hesiod, unmatched by comedians and tragedians of later days. Eurydice was his great love. She danced as beautifully as her lover sang and played; she danced with nymphs, and these forest deities preferred the Orphic songs to those of Apollo himself. As she was dancing with them in the forest, Eurydice was bitten by a snake and died. Orpheus sang songs of melancholy that moved even the oldest of the gods: the earth shook, the doors to hell were opened, and Orpheus descended into the realm of the dead in search of Eurydice. Charming the monsters, demons, and lost souls with his music, Orpheus descended until he reached Hades himself. Even the god of the dead was moved by the Orphic complaint: *Mortal silence, vain hope, what suffering, what torment, for I have lost my Eurydice.* The King of Hell granted her release. Eurydice would return to the surface with her lover, but only if Hades's stipulations were followed: Orpheus would lead her back the way they came, walking in front of her, and if he turned to look at her, she would be thrust back into the underworld. During the meandering journey back to the surface, Orpheus's joy faded into suspicion. He could not hear Eurydice's footsteps. When he reached behind, careful not to turn his head, he could not feel her. Was she following, or had Hades tricked him? Just as he crossed the threshold, he turned back to look at her. But Eurydice was still standing on other side, and was sucked back into the Underworld. Orpheus sang more sadly and more beautifully after losing Eurydice a second time, but now, his song was not met with the same sympathy. Zeus, afraid that he would share the secrets of the underworld with mortals, struck him with a thunderbolt that propelled him back into the court of Hades. The muses then took his lyre and placed it in the heavens. The lyre is the story's most important symbol, the metaphysical conceit that structures the whole myth. Playing the lyre is a kind of artifice, a practical knowledge among the forms of *techné*, the trick of human reason that lets us think that the world is ours. Orpheus is as sure of his lyre and his song as we are of our machines. Orpheus the artificer leads the way, while Eurydice, the wisdom of the heart embodied, follows him out of the darkness. But even if wisdom lets itself be led by artifice, it still cannot be grasped fully. Try to define what is most real, and it disappears. At the most basic level, we must simply trust that things are what they are—that is, trust the dark, inscrutable chthonic gods.

105

And why should we, Orphic technicians that we are, masters of the domain of the rational, put our trust in Hades and his underlings? Read the myth again: *don't look* at where Eurydice comes from, and there she is. But turn around to stare at the hellish depths from which she came, and not only will she disappear, but you will be punished by the gods for looking at things that no mortal should see. Behind every sound proposition, every simple affirmation, every banal sentence, lurks a whole series of unstable factors. For even if our thoughts seem to appear all at once, they have in fact made a slow journey towards the surface. In the fleeting instant before predicate "b" safely arrives at subject "a," everything is fluid. Lurking beneath the rational is the irrational, under the sanity of our language, the madness of the pre-linguistic. Ask any philosopher: *he knows* that there are pre-linguistic conditions for our rational speech. But he cannot tell you what they are. Look for the conditions of the rational world, and they disappear, like Eurydice, into the dark depths.

106

The Abyss. Having led the life of an itinerant scholar for two decades, the alchemist Zeno, protagonist of Marguerite Yourcenar's *The Abyss* (*L'Oeuvre au noir*, 1968), settles into what the author calls "the immobile life." Learned in the arts of healing, he takes on the role of doctor at a hospice attached to a convent of Franciscans. Living under an assumed name (Sebastian Theus—telling: it is a name for a martyred god), he occupies a small room in the convent and ferries between the little clinic and his spartan room. Under the name of Zeno, he was the author of treaties both medical and alchemical, vizier to the Sultan of Hadrianopolis, and then court physician to the King of Sweden. He had since succeeded in obscuring his own existence, living an everyman life. *Non habet nomen proprium,* he says to himself, amazed not that he could live as another, but that it was possible for him to embody any name at all; he was a nobody, a no-one whose mirror reflection does not correspond to anybody in the real world. In his little cell in the Franciscan convent, he neither worked nor read nor prayed. Instead, he performed a strange kind of alchemy on his own soul. Entering into himself, he attempted, by means of absolute concentration and utter physiological control, to separate himself from his thoughts. The very act of thinking, its genesis, its movement, now interested him more than the products of thought. Suspended in this nowhere between thinking and thought, stillness and movement, breath and word, he threw himself (*s'abîmer*) into this spiritual exercise as a mystic into God. "Threw," of course, is not the word. The French *s'abîmer* comes from *abîme*, "abyss." When one throws oneself into an ocean of contemplation, one abysses oneself. But the abyss—and Roland Barthes says this exquisitely in reference to the lover's inability to express his love in a satisfying way—is *nowhere*: "When I abyss myself, it is because there is no place for me anywhere, not even in death." The abyss is not the death that comes at life's end, nor is it the foundations of life. Not *Grund*, to speak the language of the German philosophers, but *Abgrund*, total indifference. Not the death that follows life, but the non-foundation of life that is the stillness before all movement, the mineral unconsciousness for which the death drive yearns. And so as Zeno lays on his cot in his monastery and performs the breathing exercises that the Dervish Eyoub had taught him, he is not transforming his mind into a blank slate (as if such a thing were possible!). Rather, he is performing a complex activity that moves both backwards and forwards, towards the annihilating end that resembles the indifferent beginning. He knew from alchemy what he was doing: this operation is the *solve et coagula*, the rending apart of what seems inseparable by forcing the invisible divisions that lie at the heart of all things. This grand spiritual work, this *opus nigrum*, is ultimately a preparation for meeting one's fate. Having intuited in himself the most profound kind of nothingness, Zeno can throw himself into a different kind of abyss: the inquisitor's bonfire and the hangman's noose.

107

But perhaps I should not have told you about the abyss. You may be tempted to perform your own kind of spiritual alchemy, and you may wind up with a hunk of lead—or worse. Casting yourself into an abyss—even if it is only by means of going about Dervish Eyoub's simple exercises with too much fervor—can be dangerous. You cannot stare at the no-thing that is behind the veneer of things as if it were some-thing. And if you do, it may drive you mad. Zeno undertakes his exercise very delicately, and knows what is coming. So does Hans Castorp, who spends seven years in a sanatorium, on a *magic mountain*, living the horizontal life, having philosophical debates and preparing to cast himself into the abyss of the Great War. Both characters are acting out a *mise-en-abîme*, a felicitous literary term that indicates a play-within-a-play. Zeno and Hans are both performing a sort of work of art within their own souls, and these are the driving moments in the novels to which the characters belong. But there is a more brutal possibility: in *Moby Dick*, the cabin boy Pip falls overboard into the vast ocean, and after his rescue, goes mad. He has not seen anything in particular—certainly not the whale!—but only the nothing of the abyssal waters. He was thrust into the abyss with no artifice, no technique, no guide, and the brutal encounter left him with a sort of holy wisdom, a madness that sees clearly but cannot speak. Be careful, lest you become like the madman who went looking for the secrets of the world: "The deep well knows,/Once all were deep and silent,/Everyone knew it./The deep well surely knows;/Bending over, a man understood it,/Captured it and then lost it,/Spoke madness and sang ."

108

The last time I saw J.L., he was in a strange state. The eminent scholar, author of a dozen monographs, could no longer engage in conversation. His sentences would descend from perfect coherence to archetypal babbling, a random mixture of words he had used his whole life: "The last time we spoke, we were talking about...Babylon... Kublah Khan...the decline of the Byzantines...hmm-mmm." And when his thoughts had been fully unravelled, he seemed able to return to the conversation again, and would speak normally. "I am suffering from a necrosis of the brain," he explained to me, "a side effect from last year's successful cancer treatments. Certain cells in my head have died and cannot be regenerated because the arteries are occluded. There are dark spots in my mind. If thoughts move in the wrong direction, they go beyond the limit of what I can still think, and descend into the irrational. There are small islands of irrationality within...Alexander the Great, the Seleucid Empire, three lost books by Aristotle, indeed..."

109

Melancholia VII. The melancholic's problem, of course, is that he thinks too much. As in Dürer's portrait, the thinker who is given over to withdrawal, contemplation, introversion, esoteric philosophy and theology, magic and grief grows heavy-headed. Saturn has no precious stone associated with it—only lead. Every alchemical operation begins with lead, heaviest and most worthless of metals, and when successful, ends with lead as its by-product, its *caput mortuum*. Living in Saturn's shadow, the thinker is ponderous, his *pondum* or weight is Saturnine lead, hung around his neck. But there is something to be said for this heavy-headedness. This weight, this solidity, holds his thoughts together, and keeps them from flying away. But leaden thoughts that sink will get us nowhere: real thinking is not some inert piece of rock. Just as the alchemist begins with lead but discards the leaden by-product, so, too, should the night-thinker retain the precious metal that comes out of melancholia, rather than remaining congested and weighed down.

110

Nordic nocturn. One walks through the winter landscape of Helsinki with a sense of fairy-tale uncanniness. In those darkest days of the year, when the sun sets in the middle of the afternoon, things seem to sit on the edge of infinity. The conical outcroppings of the *Jugendstil* buildings, the austere Lutheran Churches, the old trollies cutting through the snow all exhibit a kind of endless decline, a *fin-de-siècle* deterioration measured not in time but space: to the south lie glacial waters; to the east there is the vastness of Russia; to the north, there are the red pines of Karelia, and then nothing at all. In an old-fashioned restaurant near the Orthodox cemetery, a cheap buffet with stodgy food, dark beer, and long tables, I sit next to an old woman. She speaks passably good English, and, she tells me, even better Russian. We talked about life in the depth of Helsinki winter. Even if the angular cheeks, ethereal skin, and cerulean eyes of its denizens give them an angelic appearance, the Finns are a sad people. The encroachment of darkness leads to introspection, endless introspection leads to melancholy. Melancholy and darkness feed off each other until spring comes—and still, the violent brightness of Finnish spring is like another kind of darkness, a white darkness. Never does it occur to one to say, "this too shall pass, tomorrow is another day." Everything happens *sub specie aeternitatis*, amplified by the impression that it will never end. Many find it unbearable. My interlocutor told me—with a scurrilous smile—that while Finnish salaries are some of the highest in the world, so, too is their suicide rate. When the intimacy of darkness seems to stretch on forever, when new days seem infinitely far off, existence becomes unbearable. My new friend, however, with her ageless Finnish face that had seen a thousand eternal winters, reminded me that to kill yourself is no solution. You cannot wrest yourself from the dark; you can only go through it and come out the other side.

III

Dante's Beatrice, Kierkegaard's Regine, Hardenberg's Sophie. The thinker of symbols and dreams, like the Mesopotamian hierophant, always seems to have some sacrificial victim on his conscience. They all interpreted the fables of their own lives too literally, a mistake that made both the poets (and the women) suffer needlessly. Goethe had a better grasp of how to move through the play-within-a-play that is one's own life—and how to write convincing female characters. Mignon and Gretchen come and go ethereally. Are they alive or dead, still part of the story or killed off? As the action progresses, one never knows. But they always come back in the end, revealing themselves to have been a hidden centripetal force. The baroque plots of the Goethean drama are in fact literature's most effective expressions of freedom seen from within, the freedom that exists whenever two people come together. The Other disappears when idolized, only to reappear later in some surprising new form: *Das Ewig-Weibliche zieht uns hinan.*

112

Melancholia VIII. Melancholy, like the Night, is a prism through which Time is splayed out. No tolling or ticking can measure the space from darkest night to dawn. Time, called *Chronos*, and Saturn, *Kronos*, are inescapably confused, different people but one god. So, at any rate, in the spirit of the melancholic. His ponderous nature makes all moments eternal. If something has been repeated, it becomes a habit. If habit, then it has always been so. Here lies the reason for the identification of the acedia of the Church Fathers with melancholy. For Saturn, even what is new is merely repetition of the same. What exists is already there, but it never ceases to come forth anew, though always as it was before. The acediast who longs for a place that is always beyond, ever on a winter's journey, is merely conceiving of Saturn's repetitions according to space rather than time. This, perhaps, is why travel was the nineteenth century's most popular cure for melancholy. The genius of the cure lies not so much in its destination (Italy like Goethe or Russia like Rilke?) but in its very form: to travel, one must decide to leave, and decide where. The problem of Saturnine repetition is that it loses sight of the radical moment of the decision. Repetition is only a false beginning, the obfuscation of a form of idolatry—because we repeat, things must have *always* been that way. This is a lie. There *was* a beginning, and it came from a decision. All that is necessary is to retrieve it.

113

I found A.S., the great scholar of Proust, just as I had left him several years before: impeccably dressed, ensconced in the corner seat of a café, pontificating to a group of handsome young men. They were discussing whether one should begin reading *In Search of Lost Time* at the beginning, with the first volume, or somewhere in the middle. A particularly bright young person suggested that one could begin with any of the seven volumes, but was ignored. "With Proust, the beginning is not really the beginning," said A.S. "If there is a *beginning*, then it can only be the death of Albertine. After that, motion and time begin: Marcel travels to Venice, the characters begin to age. The social order is upended by a series of baffling marriages. And Marcel's own illness will demolish his high-society fantasy world. With the death of Albertine, a time of solitude begins, a foundational solitude. 'Albertine will never come back. Existence is solitary, we exist alone.' And this solitude is the beginning of the narrator's life as a writer. Have you ever realized that solitude escapes our perception, our experience, our language? We are in relation to others from the very beginning, we are already in the web of otherness in the womb. In order to be alone, to be just me, something has to die, some form of otherness has to end."—One of the young men spoke: "So the right place to start with Proust is with the first volume, but after having read the whole thing once before?"—"Yes," said A.S.—"That sounds like a very long and very lonely thing to do," said the young man.

114

La solitude originaire. Caught up in the everyday, surrounded by others, we have the impression of being continuously in relation. From the moment we awake, we are engaged in the constant commerce of otherness: bedfellows and breakfast mates; lovers and spouses; strangers and acquaintances. When we lie in bed at night, exhausted from the onslaught of otherness, it seems to us we were born alone, in an originary solitude, like Adam in his garden, and then through a lifelong succession of encounters, bound up in a web of relations, a system of otherness. Then ensues the trickiness of systematicity: when one lives inside of a system, one cannot so easily get out of it—nor even conceive of the possibility of there being something outside of it without engaging in a real feat of imagination. But if one does manage to navigate the labyrinthine system of otherness and come out—in a hermitage, a desert island, or some deep inner part of the soul where one can be alone with oneself—then one has transcended a limit, and everything appears differently. If one bursts out of the system of engrossed otherness, one sees that one was in it from the beginning: in the womb with the mother, at her breast, at play with other children, and so forth. We are not Adam, we are Eve: we come from another. We are threads that pass through the spinning wheel that shapes the web of otherness. Solitude is not originary; solitude is an achievement of spirit, a cerulean height up to which we rise. To be really alone is to perpetrate an act of violence, of negation, of extracting myself from the web. Then, one is confronted with a challenge: remain in this ecstasy of aloneness, half god and half beast, or return to the system of otherness not merely as a thread in a web, but as an individual who opens up to other individuals. That is where real otherness occurs, a kind of relation that overcomes the infantile terminology of "self" and "other." Then, one is able to inhabit the inner world of another, and reciprocally, open up one's inner world to that person, all while reserving a dark corner for oneself, a place where no other can trespass (or better still, from which no other could return). These two people would together simultaneously inhabit the cerulean heights of aloneness and the labyrinth of otherness. They would not be lovers, but, as Rilke says so well, the guardians of each others' solitude.

115

"Tender beloved—Lovely sun of the night!" The short life of Friedrich von Hardenberg was radically transformed in the space of fifteen minutes, when he saw Sophie von Kühn for the first time. She is twelve, Hardenberg twenty-two. He courts her assiduously, and while she is initially reticent, they become engaged on her thirteenth birthday, in secret. Almost immediately after, Sophie falls ill. Two years of agony ensue. Her lungs fail her, her liver weakens. She endures three cruel surgeries that are of no help. Sophie dies of tuberculosis on the eve of her fifteenth birthday. Distraught, Hardenberg plans to kill himself. What would be more fitting than a reunion of these ideal lovers in the afterlife, where the body is transformed into the stuff of the infinite? He will instead pass through the crucible of mourning and write a short text, the *Hymns to the Night*, under the pseudonym Novalis. But perhaps you are not the romantic type, and the sickly-sweet aromas of opium, chivalry, and consumption have you retching. You might be even more discouraged by the uncanny resemblance between Dante's Beatrice and Novalis's Sophie, a macabre instance of life imitating art. It would not have been lost on the poet, often accused of idealizing the Middle Ages. Of course, there can be no Novalis without the death of Sophie—only a student named Hardenberg, the son of a salt mine owner and avid reader of philosophy whose attraction to a country nymphet sways between anachronism and perversion. But the two poets inhabit

different spheres: Dante's world is a web of meaning, and to win back the lost Beloved, he need only follow the right thread, indicated by the poetic ancestor who serves as his guide. Hardenberg lives in a world untethered; the new poets search in vain for the Absolute, finding only things. The only hope of retrieving his Beloved is by plunging into the empty space between the unconnected things of the world. He must pass through this land with no horizon, no past, no future, no beginning and ending in order to find her, with no indication of where she is. Where beginnings and endings are lost, there is no "other side" to the inferno. The night itself is at once guide, destination, and place of transformation. This passage into night is not a smooth one: it is a *salto mortale*, a deathly jump—or so it seems when considered from the logical realm of daylight. This deathly jump is really a violent reversal in perspective. If the Poet-Narrator of the *Hymns to the Night* begins by longing for light in the darkness, an illumination that will cure his solitude, he soon comes to see this darkness as a space of transformation, a radical opening of the self to what is completely other: the beloved who was lost, confined to the past, and the transformed beloved of the future, the object of longing. Both womb and bridal chamber, this space between two vanishing horizons (love lost and love regained) comes to be strongly identified with the Beloved herself. Slowly, the Poet is freed from his crass daytime objectification of a poor country girl. The mediating beloved comes to be merged not only with the place of the night, but with the figure of the Christ, Novalis's archetypal night-man, he who gains life by laying it down. Both the opacity of darkness and the dreamless slumber that is death cease to be absolute limitations, and instead become unfathomable places of transformation, passageways into a higher life whose possibilities are not limited by the logic that governs things. Hardenberg's world is filled with objects and fetishes that pass away; Novalis creates a world filled with real people who are to come.

116

ἔκστασις. Who am I? If you have spent much time mulling over this question, you have fallen under the spell of the philosophers, especially that ugly gadfly who wanders around the Agora all day. I will not discourage you from these frequentations—somehow, I cannot bring myself to hate old Socrates; he is charming, if sometimes disingenuous. All while pestering you with the refrain, *know yourself!* he is keeping a secret from you. When he asks himself this question, he does not stay with the confines of "myself." There is a spirit within him that is greater than he is, a spirit with one foot in the heavens and one on earth. All of Socrates's wisdom comes from the secret conversations he has with his inner spirit, his *daimon*. He is at once himself and not himself, within himself and beyond himself, here and somewhere else. But here is the real secret: that is precisely what it means to be *yourself*, and it is only in looking for yourself that you will find your daimon. Then, you will realize that this daimonic existence is the real meaning of what it is *to be*: to stand outside of oneself, to exist beyond oneself. We live in ecstasy, or not at all.

117

"One, two, three...where is the fourth?" Socrates is counting his dinner guests. One has taken ill, and cannot come. No matter. When it comes to counting, getting to three already provides satisfaction. There is a mysticism of counting, an esoteric meaning to it. Today, Socrates has no speech to give. And neither does Hermocrates. Critias will only say a few words, a little story as *hors d'oeuvre* before the mathematical feast. No, they are content to learn to count. And they have brought a young Pythagorean to teach them, a disciple of the triangle mystics, the masters of three. Listen carefully to the young Timaeus as he speaks. He will tell us how the world was created, who made it and out of what sort of stuff. *One.* Being, the eternal, that which is grasped by the mind. *Two,* Becoming, what comes into existence and passes away, which is grasped by the senses. These are the two things that form the world. It is an animal with a body and soul, one living thing with two aspects. But how are its two elements to be brought together? Being is the stuff of the mind, becoming the stuff of the body. The god who made the world needed a third thing in order to combine them. This third thing would have to be a container for being and becoming, a neutral element that sustains their meeting, combining, and being shaped into the stuff of the world. Being, the first thing, is known by the mind. Becoming, the second, by the senses. But how can we know the container, the frame, the place of transformation that is the unifying third? We hardly know it, and when we do, it is through a kind of bastard reasoning (*logismoi nothoi*). The bastard has an Athenian father and an alien mother; one foot in the city, one in an unknown place. To think in this way is to give the imagination free reign; to let things that might have been and that cannot be enter into the space where being and becoming meet. In imagination, we intuit the shape-shifting third thing, the chameleon being that takes on the shape of whatever it represents. To know it is to imagine all its shapes, and then wait for one to be realized.

118

Perchance to dream VII. There is a curious moment in Cicero's philosophical dialogue, *On the Republic*. The entire sixth book of the text takes the form of a dream sequence in which Scipio Aemilianus is guided through a series of fanciful visions by his late grandfather, the great general of the Punic Wars, Scipio Africanus. Bringing him up to starry heights, the elder Scipio tells his grandson's future. If the young man stays faithful to his duties, he will spend eternity even higher up, in the highest heavens that the sages of Greece have described. Looking down, the younger Scipio sees Rome, and this, the greatest city ever built by human hands, looks insignificant compared to the city of stars above him. He is then guided by his grandfather through the firmament, and level after level, star after star, the order and movement of the heavens is explained to him. He hears the most divine music, and is told by his guide that this is the music of the spheres, the consoling sounds that the even the greatest Greek philosophers could only theorize. Now, taken up into the sky, they are far enough away from the din of earthly affairs to hear it properly. This astral projection, modelled on the myth of Er in Plato's *Republic*, is occasion for Cicero to recount the Stoics' exquisite conception of the universe, as impressive a cosmology as those of the Platonists and Aristotelians, in a sensual rather than discursive medium. Cicero's account is so evocative that it invites exploration. Macrobius's *Commentary on the Dream of Scipio*, a madcap work, is less a commentary than a circumambulation. In examining the dream, he discourses on the nature of the soul, the movements of the stars, and the mathematical beauty of music. This commentary on a commentary (Plato's *Republic*, Cicero's *Republic*, Macrobius's dream-book) is full of long quotations from platonic philosophers. Macrobius is less the author of a text than he is the dreamer of a dream; his dream-world is peopled by sacred proportions, philosophical intuitions, and mythological figures. It lends itself well to visual representations, and the middle ages see a proliferation of Macrobean spherical diagrams. The curious scholar will find a fine collection of these in the Danish Royal Library. But do not look for me there. I will be in the National Gallery in London, admiring Raphael's *Vision of a Knight*, sometimes called *The Dream of Scipio*. In it, Aemilianus slumbers under a tree as two female figures watch over him: they are Virtue and Pleasure. His countenance radiates a meditative peace. We cannot know what visions fill his soul. His dreams are his own.

119

Voluptuaries of sleep IV. Before H*** became a lover of sleep, he was a lover of the baser pleasures to be found in bed, sometimes dispensing with the bed altogether. Still, he liked to repeat that there was nothing that could not be done in bed. Those were days of astounding productivity for my sybarite friend. Often, I would walk into a Paris hotel room (just as a different kind of companion was leaving) to find him lying down, smoking cigarettes and writing furiously. In those days he wrote much and slept little, his nights a collage of books, lovers, cigarettes, and cognac. Book succeeded book, and his reputation grew to oracular heights: he was translated into Persian, Arabic, and Urdu, and collected obscene sums in exchange for improvised lectures in Dubai and Rabat. I occasionally accompanied him, and occasionally took notes, hoping to write a review for some magazine or other, but those were days when I wrote little and went to bed early. Our friendship was reduced to meetings in restaurants, usually near the hotels where H*** was able to continue his furiously horizontal existence. It was very gradually that a change began to take place. My days lengthened, and his shortened. I began to work, to write, to haunt libraries and stay until late. I could not—cannot—sleep; I learned that genuine thoughts are night-thoughts, and would come, intrusively, in the dark. H***, on the other hand, has not published a book in almost a decade. His quest for wisdom was replaced with the quest for finding the best bed in Paris. His long nights were now filled with oneiric delights. At our last meeting, H***, one of the greatest orientalists of our generation, spoke to me of the concept of the *badaliya*, or spiritual substitute. And perhaps some oriental curse was placed on us to that effect: before, I slept and kept silent so he could write; now, we have reversed roles.

120

I've been told you're looking for a teacher, and that you'll pay handsomely for lessons... I am sure there is some sophist whose eye twinkles as he imagines the sterling coins, and would teach you for as many hours as you want. It is my duty, however, to lift the veil, and tell you the teacher's secret: no one ever taught anyone else, there is no teaching, and there is—at least in this particular sense—no learning either. There is only a kind of remembering. You may not be convinced, but Socrates is on my side, you see, and was himself against all teaching. Meno's slave boy, for example, learned geometry not from Socrates's lessons, but from Socrates drawing the knowledge out of him, showing him knowledge that he had forgotten. Of course, one only recalls what is essential. What is contingent passes from memory with death and rebirth; new life is a clean slate, one that thrusts the oldest truths deep into the soul. To know, to recall what is essential, is a spiritual affair, an active way of purifying the soul of what is sensuous, contingent, and untrue. The path of purification, of *catharsis,* is memory, *anamnesis.* But how does one go about this exercise? Dante, the secret Platonist, teaches us. At the summit of Mount Purgatory, Dante reaches the entrance to the earthly paradise, the place where his oldest ancestors lived in blissful ignorance. In order to enter the garden, he must be cleansed of his sins. In the river Lethe he is washed, and both his sins and his memory of ever having committed them are removed. He says to Beatrice, his angelic guide, that he does not remember having ever been estranged from her absolute purity. She smiles, and says to him: Recall that today, you drank from the river Lethe. Your sins have been forgotten, but you are still a sinner. Remember, at least, that you have forgotten!

121

Speaking of religion: memory is more resurrection than preservation. The resurrected man of the Gospels is not immediately recognizable; he does not look like the person he was before. His body shines with celestial beauty, even if it still bears the marks of torture. Scorched by his descent into hell, he smells both of sulphur and the sea.

122

Lights, camera, action. In the past half-century, the novel has undergone an inconceivable transition. The culprits, it would seem, are French writers who fell under the spell of film directors. The *nouvelle vague* gave birth, in secret, to a bastard child, the *nouveau roman*. Held hostage in seedy movie theaters, the novel became not only visual, but utterly cinematographic. Pick up any book with a glossy new cover, open it to any page, and you will see what I mean. Not only does visual description reign ("the lamp was on the upper-left-hand corner of the table. There was a round mark left by its previous position, on the table's lower right..."), but scenes are visually composed as in a film. Indeed, the word "scene" is already a betrayal, suggesting that a novel is nothing other than a film projected onto the mind's eye. In nearly every novel we read, the cinematographers are at work, and the cameras are zooming in and out. Our writers have come down with iconophilia, the most common perversion among those who sleep with the lights on. It ignores that the literary is its own category, quite apart from the purely visual. What would become of Proust or Mann or Joyce, Balzac or Dickens or Fontane, if their accounts of the inner life were flattened into a visual medium? Theirs is a literature that is completely musical, soul-symphonies in words. Homer, as legend would have it, was blind. This legend gives us the litmus test for really great writers: can you tell your story in the dark?

123

As I examine my strange little collection of fragments, I wonder if some magnificent adding machine, the descendant of Leibniz's Stepped Reckoner or the Pascaline, might not be able to write just as good a book. The fragment, after all, is tailored to the machine ghost writer, who could surely imitate a short, incomplete piece of miscellany. The more a book resembles *art trouvé*, the easier the task for artificial imitators. But writers of fat paragraphs and thick tomes are not immune. The book, especially the scholarly book, has become sclerotic, so formulaic and predictable, that any machine worth its minerals could imitate the pedantic five-chapter dissertation, itself a pastiche of something much freer. The book of the future will have to be something very different. Every book will have to be absolutely personal, a love letter or nothing at all. This is all books ever were to begin with—what Jean Paul calls "fat letters to friends."

124

Melancholia IX. A stranger I came, a stranger I leave. This is the symphonic complaint that begins Franz Schubert's song cycle the *Winter's Journey*. We hear one voice for the hour that the cycle lasts, that of a musician whose proposal was spurned by the woman he loved. The spring had been good to him, and the stranger had found some acceptance in his adopted community: his beloved had become his betrothed. A sudden reversal then casts him out; the engagement is mysteriously broken off, and he is reminded that he remains a stranger in that place. There is nothing left for him but to leave. This feeling of alienation, of deep *Entfremdung*, is the romantic's most serious affliction, a melancholic complication of acedia. The irony or self-distancing that characterizes the romantic intellect is amplified; the particular experience that occasioned the alienation and caused one to flee quickly develops into self-alienation. In the case of our wandering musician, he leaves town at night, careful not to wake up his beloved. The winter weather is harsh; the wind and weathervanes seem to mock him, his tears freeze, and he seeks in vain amidst the snow not only a footprint of his beloved, but some sign of spring. By the middle of the cycle, the passage from alienation to self-alienation has been completed; gone is the dream of the beloved, and in its place are the enormous symbols of death and spring, held together in impossible tension. The tension reaches a deceptively tranquil high point with the simple quatrains of a song called *The Inn* (*Das Wirtshaus*). The wanderer has actually come to a graveyard where all the plots are taken. This is the "cool inn" where Spring and Death meet. In this world from which he is alienated, there is no one to offer him hospitality, not even death. Our last image of the wanderer is of his meeting with a street musician on the edge of the town where the graveyard was. The man is an assemblage of paradoxes. He is a musician who is no musician, since he merely turns the crank of his hurdy-gurdy, which emits a sound that is hardly music. He is a beggar who stands outside of the town where prospective benefactors live, and there are no coins in his little plate. It is winter, but he is barefoot on the ice. He merely lets the world do what it will, and keeps on cranking his little instrument, producing the same monotonous sounds that people ignore and that makes dogs bark, over and over. *Will you accompany my songs?* The wanderer asks him. And they both fade away into the winter night.

125

In the beginning, God created the heavens and the earth. This old account of the beginning of all things, of their *arché*, as the Greek translation would have it, is the most obscure of all stories. For it is not a story that is told by a poet, the invention of some bard. Rather, this story of the origins of all things is older than the poet's craft. In the beginning... this is a story that gives birth to poets, the story out of which poets and their tales emerge, since it is the absolute beginning of all things. It means (or so the theologians tell us) that God created everything out of nothing, *ex nihilo*. But how are we to understand this *nothing*? The theologians cannot tell us, and we must wander down the shady streets of Amsterdam's Jewish quarter, past crowded market stalls where the smells of spice, leather and rot assail the nostrils, through narrow alleyways and pandemonium thoroughfares, until we reach the Portuguese synagogue. In a hidden room in its attic (not altogether different from the place where the Golem is hidden in Prague), a place that resembles a carpenter's workshop more than a scholar's study, a master of the Kabbalah waits for us. His secret science is not for everyone, but only those persistent enough to find him. His doctrine is as elusive as his hiding place, for what he teaches is *nothing*. This is one of the most essential aspects of the Kabbalah, going back to its initiator, rabbi Isaac Luria, and his spiritual heir, Chaim Vital. In a passage from his *Etz Chaim*, Vital informs us that before the emanations were emanated and the creations created, there existed pure simple light, infinite and self-same, the very being of the Holy One. In order to create that which is different from himself, the Holy One had to *contract* his light, to pull it back into the center, making space for what is other. This movement of contraction, the *tzimtzum*, is the great paradox of creation, one that the canonical text of Genesis runs over roughshod: the first things that God makes are not heaven and earth; this is a title, a proleptic announcement, not a moment in the argument. Nor is it *light*, for light belongs to God—it is his speech. God is a God of words, and his people, the Jews, are people of words and books. God has always been speaking. Without words, there is no God, and without God, there are no words. His words are his light, which he speaks eternally. And so the first moment of creation is the creation of the Nothing, the empty space in which all other things come to be. Perhaps you have heard this elsewhere, in a more western idiom. For the kabbalistic wisdom was stolen by a promethean Jewish philosopher, expelled from the Portuguese synagogue. *Omnis determinatio est negatio,* writes Baruch Espinosa. Did he know that he was echoing the secret teachings of Luria? The rabbis of the Portuguese synagogue surely did. And they knew also that this was the secret of words, the secret of books. For to write is to restrain, to choose one's words, to carefully form letters. Writing is always an act not just of omission (and indeed, in classical Hebrew script, the vowels are always omitted), but of *erasure*. God created the world by restraining his word; he created the world by erasing. All creating is writing, all writing comes from erasing. As Blanchot puts it: "Everything must be erased, everything will be erased. It is because of the Infinite need for erasure that writing takes place and has its place."

126

My greatest vice? Gluttony, and not just for books. I have partaken in sumptuous meals: deconstructed dishes; sliced and presented duck breasts, those insatiable ducks with their swollen livers; oysters glistening and metallic; burnished burgundies breathing icy fruit aromas. They come to memory in fragments, in small moments that one might call courses. A course is a synecdoche, a short moment that refers to a whole. The unifying thread of all these courses is the guests who partake in them. One never says, do you remember when we ate such-and-such a dish? but rather, do you remember when so-and-so came to dinner? The memory of the meal is the true host. Here, then, is another meaning of the word *anamnesis*, another aspect of remembrance. The Christian ritual of the Lord's meal is nothing other than a calling-to-mind of the supper, an illumination of the faces of those who broke bread together.

127

For your edification. On a dreary evening up at the Berghof, as the humanist-belletrist Settembrini and the nihilist-jesuitical Naphta argue, Mme Chauchat relaxes her flabby-asiatic form into her wicker chair, and blows smoke in Hans Castorp's face. "How reassuring to hear that at least *you*, Herr Castorp," she says, nodding demurely in the direction of the debate next to them, "are not a passionate man. Passion is what is for itself, life for life's sake, a forgetting of oneself. It is not serious. But you Germans are perhaps *too* serious. You are only interested in experience, in doing things in order to build yourselves up with experience. Some day you will unleash all your experience, and destroy the world." This sentiment is not far away from Schopenhauer's diatribe against reading in *Parerga and Paralipomena.* When we read, someone else thinks for us, he intones. But Schopenhauer is not against books any more than Mme Chauchat is against experience (indeed, isn't the Berghof itself an extravagant horizontal experience?). In Schopenhauer's case, he is against reading out of snobbism, reading secondary works rather than great literature itself, and against the wanton writing of books, and the wanton neglect of great books: who could not cry, he writes, when one thinks that the colossal catalogue of the Leipzig University Library's new acquisitions is almost entirely composed of works that will be completely forgotten in ten years' time? No, the object of Schopenhauer's ire is reading as an accessory, reading as something external to one's own soul, reading as a mere technology. If reading is inner experience, one need only broaden the argument to all experience to arrive at Clawdia Chauchat's argument: I build myself up with experience, I become an efficient machine, and then I do what all machines do when unchecked by human spirit: destroy. Remember, my dear Hans, that *Bildung,* your German word for culture comes from Bild, to make something in the image of something greater, not the English *build*!

128

Ever since I have known him, Professor A.C. has been mad. As all madness does, it began as an innocent obsession tinged with a note of darkness. Ten years my senior, A.C. was already assistant to the illustrious Herr Professor Doktor B*** when I first arrived in Tübingen. Rather than working on his Habilitation, A.C. was engrossed in writing an epic poem in Ancient Greek. He would sit in a little tavern on the edge of town, half-hidden by a mountain of rumpled papers, and as students and old men drank white wine and made merry, A.C. worried about his hexameters. His passion for the Greek poets transcended both history and geography, and he would occasionally mistake the *Biergarten* for the Athenian portico, or call the lecture hall the amphitheater. I was reunited with my eccentric friend at a conference—a kind of gathering that I rarely attend—after many years of separation. At lunch on the first day, he took me aside. His breath stunk of coffee and schnapps. "I must prepare you for my talk," he said. "I will be revealing a great mystery. I have discovered the secret language of the Phoenician settlers of the island of Samothrace. It is the key to the ancient religion that they practiced, a cult that was already a myth in the time of Plato. I made the long journey to the island by ship last spring so that I could summon their gods, the Kabiri. Their names have not been evoked for millennia. I returned to the mainland transformed. Nothing can be the same now." A.C.'s presentation that afternoon was a slide show of pictures from a holiday on a Greek island, taken with his wife some years before. The pictures, mostly of random objects on ferries and in tourist restaurants, were blurry and hastily snapped. I did not believe for one moment that he had a wife. As the pictures succeeded each other on the screen, A.C.'s colleagues, who had slowly grown used to his folly like frogs to boiling water, ruffled their papers or read books they had brought. I was the only one who sat unprepared, and was forced to meditate on how my old acquaintance's soul had descended into obscurity.

129

Through a glass, darkly. If we could see the world as if through sound-proofed glass, watching its pantomime, we would know *that* life is, and finally see the enormity of such a that.

130

Socrates worried that writing would destroy our memories and dampen our intellects. His worry is facetious—for it is Plato who puts these words in his mouth, and does it not only in writing, but in one of the most beautifully written works of the ancient Greek language. Let me be your Socrates then, and make his point with no hint of irony. Your teachers, engrossed in the contemporary, were almost certainly enemies of memorization. To memorize is worthless, they say, what is important is *putting knowledge to use*. But what will happen when wars and catastrophes come, when the soldiers commandeer the academies, burn the books, and throw the teachers in prison? It happens frequently in human history. It is happening today. You need not look very far to see whole peoples and nations violated by barbarian hoards, their language and its literature on the brink of extinction. What knowledge will you put to use once your poets have been murdered and you have been sent into exile empty-handed? If you can still recite one poem from those books that were burned, you have not lost everything.

131

The commander closes the heavy door to his office, pulls off his long boots, and loosens his collar. He sets his hat down next to the gramophone, and chooses a record. The warm sound of the phonograph fills the room like a steam bath, and he lowers himself into the divan with a feeling of immense pleasure. On the table next to him is the leather-bound copy of the *Italian Journey* that his wife had sent from Munich. How can one imagine oneself in Sicily with Goethe when the harsh Polish winter has reached its peak, and the sun sets at three in the afternoon? From the gramophone comes the alternately warm and cold, consoling and melancholic Schubert song, "The Linden Tree." Going from major to minor, the song moves from spring to winter and back again. The transformation is subtle, and envelopes one so completely that one has the impression of being in a whirlwind: the rustling leaves yield to the piercing cold of winter wind in only a few bars. As he listened, he looked out the window and watched the great billows of smoke dance in the wind, and did not once think of what was burning.

132

Melancholia X. The night is not a time of sadness, but melancholy is its attitude. What are we to make of this paradox? We cannot simply overcome our melancholy. We must instead harness its power to be able to think in the special way that is ours. Here, our master is Marsilio Ficino. Translator of Plato and Plotinus, self-described "Platonic philosopher, doctor, theologian," Ficino had the misfortune of being melancholic both by birth, since his horoscope places Saturn in the ascendent, and by art, since those whose lives are devoted to study are prone to bouts of atrabiliousness. But unlike his predecessors, who were content to let Saturn speak and resign themselves to their fate, Ficino sought to embrace the paradoxes of the god. He was a son of Saturn, and learned the secret to harnessing its power, presenting his findings to us in a book that embodies "the magic chiaroscuro of Christian neo-Platonic mysticism." *De triplici vita* (1480–89) is a handbook "on the therapy and symptoms of the Saturnine character." But the nature of this therapy is highly original. In the Greek medical treatises with which Ficino was so familiar, the treatment that is *therapeia* is accomplished by means of *pharmakon*, a potion or elixir, or by extension a spell or incantation. Because an antidote is often derived from the poison it is meant to cure, *pharmakon* refers ambivalently to both. Ficino proceeds cautiously, knowing that for Saturn, the god who unites opposites, the antidote is not extracted from the poison: the antidote *is* the poison, and vice-versa. Melancholy is an affliction that oppresses. But it is Saturn that guides the mind toward the contemplation of things divine. Melancholics are prone to contemplating higher things, and even the most sanguine character becomes melancholic if he contemplates them assiduously enough. Ficino's *pharmakon* is a strong tincture: drink a little, and your spirit will be elevated beyond itself. Drink too much, and you will go mad, possessed by the oldest and most enthralling of all the gods.

133

A night in suite no. 10. The tap in the adjacent bathroom drips at a larghetto rhythm. From the bed, one can imagine the slow formation of water into a droplet around its mouth. Through the thin wall, one hears the grunts and little screams of theatrical love-making. From above, one hears the scratching patter of animal feet. Are dogs allowed? Analogously, there are no-smoking signs everywhere, yet the hallway still smells of stale tobacco. Lie on your side with your good ear below, and put the second pillow over your other ear. In the absence of a second pillow, use a rolled-up blanket. Press firmly, and the sounds will be dampened. Just then, the operetta love-making reaches its comical crescendo, the dog barks, toilets flush, doors slam. At precisely six a.m., the masons begin hammering at the cobblestone outside. The agony is over.

134

Melancholia XI. Ficino's threefold book on life, *De triplici vita*, bears as subtitle, "On Caring for the health of those who devote themselves to literary studies." In this way, much like Robert Burton, Ficino must write his way into his subject matter. But Ficino is craftier than Burton, whose melancholy belies a certain naivety. Burton's *Anatomy* is a labyrinthine word game that grows peripherally as the focus of the players narrows. It is an unwieldy almanac, a baggy monster, a world that contains an infinite number of other worlds, not all of which are of interest. Its Cheshire-cat-journey stands in contrast to the focused spiritual exercise that is the *Three Books on Life*. Burton is not worried about the starting point. One can start reading the *Anatomy of Melancholy* on any page: begin how and where you will. But Ficino must begin at just the right place: we start with the "antidote" of the *pharmakon*, the scholarly life, and then distill it down to the poison, melancholy, before restoring the good that is the scholarly life at its highest level, the art of contemplation. We are given not an unwieldy almanac, but a recipe book with imperatives for performing a delicate spiritual alchemy. This spiritual cookbook teaches us a dietetic of opposites: frugal gluttony, humble narcissism, blasphemous piety. It is the contradiction itself that is redemptive. We must embrace it if we are to understand Saturn as the god whose wisdom is folly and whose frenzy is sadness.

135

Umberto Eco, man of baroque dreams and fantastic histories, was given the famous Proust questionnaire on French television. Your favorite sound, Monsieur Eco? Silence. And your least favorite sound? Silence.

136

If one wanders north of Taksim, crossing Tarlabaşı boulevard, another world opens up. On the other side of this threshold, the Ottoman fairy-tale of old Istanbul fades away, and a new world—squalid, decayed, and forgotten—absorbs the visitor into its putrid bosom. Furtively, Tarlabaşı opens its arms to adventurers. Narrow streets wind steeply upward, tracing paths through crumbling Belle-Époque buildings, heaps of litter, and rusted cars. The view is buffered by endless rows of washing hung out on lines that span buildings. Innumerable cats jump from ledge to ledge, meowing, hissing, and pawing the refuse in search of food. Dark-skinned children run up and down, kicking improvised footballs with their black-soled feet. Through open windows, one sees fastidious transvestites carefully apply their rouge; enormous gypsy families in impossibly small spaces; stray dogs sleeping on abandoned mattresses, left by the evicted tenants. The midday call of the muezzin floats into all of these places, equally unheeded by all. This is not the Istanbul of blue-mosque piety, of imposing Ottoman imperialism and its many recreations, but of heresy, iconoclasm, and transgression. In the old days, this was a neighborhood of *Rum*, the Greek Orthodox descendants of the Byzantines, proud citizens of the Eastern Empire, who the Turks half-disparagingly still call *Romans*. During the long waning of the Ottoman Empire, Tarlabaşı was the taint at the heart of the Sick Man of Europe. In those days, the exiles of the world gathered in Istanbul, and they found their home in its most notorious neighborhood. Today, outcasts of every color—Jews, Armenians, Kurds, Syrian Christians, West Africans, Pashtuns, and Persians—are all to be found, standing on the same urine-stained streets and selling their broken possessions to the junk vendors on the corners, stitching a cosmopolitan quilt of decay. Decidedly, there is no romancing this place, no chic bohemian veneer can encase it. If artists and writers have sat in its attics, freezing in winter and roasting in summer, it is because exile does not spare the gifted: Nabokov lands here as he flees the Bolsheviks, Auerbach the Nazis. How were they able to write here, in this place with no books, no ink, and not a moment of silence? As I walk up and down the narrow streets, see their chaos and feel their suffering, I know that I could not get any work done here. But in this purgatorial corner of the world, so far from the gentility of my European haunts, I feel something is at work in me, something old and deep, something as ancient as Babel, where the first incomprehensible cries of suffering rose up.

137

Melancholia XII. Ficino's deceptive beginning—which has nothing to do with melancholy—is a ruse. Like Odysseus who escapes the cyclops by making puns, Ficino begins with lightness so that we do not lose heart. Indeed, the greatest contradiction we must embrace in working through our melancholy is accepting that the end is the beginning, the bottom is the top, the way up is the way down. (Of course Ficino knew the phrase from Heraclitus: the way up is the way down). In observing the movements of our own inner lives, most of us misunderstand beginnings and endings. Perhaps more precisely: we are given to separating the beginning of something and its ending as if they had no connection. Ficino sees from the start that the only way out of melancholy—indeed, the royal road that harnesses its magic—is through it. In this way, the hurdy-gurdy man that the wanderer meets at the end of the *Winter's Journey* is not death. Both death and spring have been denied at the graveyard-inn. The old man is rather an accompanist to the wanderer's songs, a sort of spirit guide who, like Dante's Virgil, can bring him down to the depths of a personal inferno. That the songs they play are at first sad and out of tune shows how deeply the two figures are allied at this moment in the journey. They have reached the icy pit of the lowest hell, where fire grows so intense that it paradoxically freezes over. Now their upward journey can begin.

138

Rabbi G***, great scholar of the Talmud and compulsive commentator, was author or editor of nearly a thousand books. "Do not ask any questions about them," the aged cleric said to me when I met him, "I have forgotten most of them." Some of his own books were as mysterious to him as the ones that had burned in the library of Alexandria.

139

The shepherd boy Endymion was so beautiful that Selene, Titan goddess of the moon, fell madly in love with him. The moon, at once reliable and magical, source of both light and madness, was infected with a new kind of folly. The face of the sleeping Endymion, caressed by moonlight as he gently breathed, so excited her that she asked Zeus to plunge him into an eternal slumber. Since Hera, his wife, was also in love with the Endymion, Zeus acquiesced—never again would the Queen of Olympus be hypnotized by those boyish looks! And so he slept at the mouth of a cave on Mount Latmos, and each night, Selene came to caress him with moonlight-fingers. She bore him fifty daughters, fifty beauties he would never admire, for his eyes remained forever shut. We moderns have lost our night, but ancient Endymion, lover of the old goddess and prisoner to sleep, dreams, and death, had lost his day.

140

The bad old songs, the bad and bitter dreams. German Romanticism did not fade gently away. It was murdered, overcome by the poison pen of its last great heir, Heinrich Heine. From the Parisian bedroom to which he was confined, writhing in pain that opium tinctures could not relieve, Heine killed off the romantic soul by turning it against itself. Irony had always been the soul of romanticism; the attitude of the new poet, who lived in a world where the Absolute was always to be sought but never found, was one of positioning oneself between world and soul, subject and object, word and meaning. In the interstices, beauty could be found and God restored. One needed to inhabit one's longings, realizing that all philosophy can only ever be a kind of homesickness. Heine directed romanticism's great weapon against it, describing the beautiful soul of the poet with an irony at once comical and scathing. In *The Book of Songs*, Heine mocks the poet's love strains, drowning him in sighs, dreams, nightingales, doves, and lilies, all of it perfumed with a faint odor of consumption. Implied (though never avowed) is that the starry-eyed poet threw himself into the Rhine, the only coffin deep enough to contain his sorrow after his beloved had been lost. The reader, observing this ridiculous love from the comfortable distance of the library armchair, is suspended between laughter and disgust—a kind of irony that is proper to Heine. Yet one famous reader of the *Buch der Lieder* is entirely oblivious to this. Robert Schumann selects sixteen poems from the collection and sets them to music. *A Poet's Love* is an entirely serious interpretation of the texts, giving absolute credibility to the May-time passion and subsequent despair of the romantic poet-protagonist. In a subtle expression of identification with the lover, Schumann begins the first song, "In the Beautiful Month of May," with a musical quotation from Clara Schumann's piano concerto in A minor. He is the poet, and his song is true. It is precisely this proximity, this absolute identification with the lover, that makes Schumann's interpretation credible—Schumann, whose beloved Clara was sometimes near, at home with him in Leipzig, and sometimes painfully far away, crisscrossing Europe as she gave recitals. His songs are at once intimate portraits, where a mere semitone can change the mood, and jarring avowals of yearning, filled with the stilted rhythm that is Schumann's natural idiom. Heine, lying in bed, drowsy from laudanum, unable to crawl to the window to watch the Parisian boulevard, stands at an ironic distance, removed from his own experience. And when one is too far removed from one's own experience, all things descend into kitsch: every love scene is comical if one stands far enough away to remain indifferent. Foregoing narrative, explanation, and above all, theory, Schumann dives into experience at a dotted eighth-note gallop. His passion for life is too earnest to admit of any irony.

141

Every fragment is an unwritten book; every book, an overworked fragment.

142

Where shall I bring you in my beloved Tarlabaşı? Even here, where night shines brighter than day, and secrets replace everyday speech, there are mysteries into which one must first be initiated. Come with me through the broken wooden door, across the abandoned room filled with rotting newspaper and inhabited by feral cats, down into the basement, strewn with mildewed mattresses and clouded by aromatic smoke. Here, you can be initiated into the vice of poets. While our basement opium den may repulse you at first, soon it will be transformed, and you will call it—as did Baudelaire, that most passionate of opium eaters—your artificial paradise. Do not be afraid, an expert *Teriyaki*, an opium-smoker straight from Teheran, will prepare your pipe. No *chinoiseries* for us: we will be smoking *à l'iranienne*: the old *Teriyaki* will place a round ball of opium in your *bafour*, the opium pipe, and use a small knife to separate it like dough, and knead it into four long strands. Then he will place it over the gentle flame of a lamp, and after it has warmed for a while, he will begin to mix the opium into a paste. You will meanwhile recline on the best mattress (the privilege of the initiate) and as you bring the flute-like stem of the pipe to your mouth, the *Teriyaki* will gently heat the bowl, and encourage you to inhale. The first-time smoker is often overcome with nausea. If you are spared this terrible suffering and can stand the bitter, smoky taste, the disquieting euphoria will begin, a sense of hovering between one's *I* and the world it inhabits, of no longer being the one who perceives, but perception itself—no longer I, but rather *eye*. Are you asleep or still awake? Does the old Iranian still appear to stand so close, or is he a dream-like vision from which you have distanced yourself? De Quincy, the most famous of opium chroniclers, puts in words what Novalis, Coleridge, Baudelaire, Berlioz and Nietzsche can only intimate in elaborate imagery: opium does not produce dreams. Rather, like the *Teriyaki* dexterously mixing the black paste in the *bafour*, it weaves the "silken garment of imagination" from threads that are already there. As you move farther and farther away as the opiate takes its full effect, and watch the weave of the imaginal, you may see some of those fantastic visions that opium-smoking poets love so dearly: stagnant waters, sunken temples, wicked succubi, floating eyes, hermetic priests—one image succeeds another, enchanting before disappearing, ceding its place to another completely engrossing phantasm. You cannot find a solid point on which to stand where the dream visions can be gathered together; no matter how far removed you are, you are always under the spell of some miniature—a vision sees you rather than the reverse. Now you have learned the blight of opium: it robs one of the whole.

143

Georges Bataille—philosopher, librarian, numismatist, pervert, intimate of the gloomiest recesses of life—felt in himself a prophetic vocation. His calling was nothing less than to found a religion. It would be a religion of headless idols, of ecstasy above transcendence, of broken trinities: the Father, like a voracious Saturn, would gobble himself up, leaving behind only refuse and shaken followers. The exoteric organ of this Dionysiac cult would be a magazine, called *Acéphale*, "the headless," and would provide Bataille's new religion with a theology (or, as it were, an a-theology). Its saints would be Dionysius, Heraclitus, the Marquis de Sade, and Don Giovanni. Its first initiate, the prophet who all were to follow, would be Nietzsche. From the philosopher of the Overman, the headless disciples would learn a mysticism of the void, an eroticism of death, and the vertiginous triumph of thinking the infinite without transcendent obstacles. The esoteric expression of *Acéphale* would be a secret society, one whose members were sworn to silence, and whose rituals included travelling at an appointed time on an appointed train to a forest where sulfur would be burned at the foot of a fallen tree; a gathering in the middle of the night during the full moon; and commemorating the beheading on Louis XVI on Place de la Concorde—there, at the foot of the obelisk, the secret death of God, his beheading, could be whispered to the adepts of this godless, headless, religion. The whole thing would collapse after Bataille suggested to his co-religionists that they engage in the ultimate conjuration, one that would forge a permanent bond between them: a human sacrifice. This would be their foundational myth, the object of their hymns and treatises forever. Bataille knelt in the forest near the burning sulphur and proclaimed that he himself would be the sacrificial victim. But none of the others would kill him, and so the secret society and the journal it inspired ceased to exist.

144

For the Ancients, Homer was not just a poet, but a theologian. All of the wisdom of the ancestors, the secret knowledge of the old gods, was to be found allegorically in the *Odyssey* and the *Iliad*. To see it, one must engage in that most venerable of philosophical activities: the commentary. Porphyry, the most gifted writer among the neoplatonists, offers us an interpretation of the *Odyssey* as a Pythagorean-Platonic fable. The whole epic is about *genesis*, a portrayal of the coming-into-being of those things subject to change. We, the philosopher-readers, are bent on transcending this to arrive at the peaceful hovering of the eternal, of what simply *is*. The blinding of the cyclops Polyphemus was a vain attempt at this transcendence, using matter to thwart the senses rather than using the mind to surpass them. The right method is instead the one announced by the blind Prophet Tiresias: learn to forget the sea, the place of strife and travels, and your forgetting of mere experience, of things in succession, will lead you up the spiritual path to what never changes. The way to enact this method is demonstrated in a key passage that Porphyry identifies—one that is marginal, confusing, and full of inconsistencies—and that he takes to be a microcosm of the whole story. Odysseus has just arrived on the shores of Ithaca, where, near the harbor, there is a cave inhabited by nymphs. In it are mixing bowls, honeybees, ever-flowing springs, and stone looms on which the nymphs weave webs of purple dye. There are two doors into the cave, on the north and south sides. The latter is only for immortals. The ship sailed in from the north, and the sleeping Odysseus was laid down on the shore. He has passed through the door reserved for mortals, and landed, in a sleep akin to death, in the land of forgetting and transformation, of the soul's passage towards the eternal. He will leave by the other door, reserved for immortals. For now, he is in the philosopher's Ithaca, the place where the sea is forgotten and the true nature of the soul remembered.

145

When he saw that Caesar's forces had become unstoppable, Cato the Younger, that great defender of traditions and constitutions, votary of the written word, took his dagger and disemboweled himself. Before he did so, says his biographer Plutarch, he read Plato's *Phaedo*, which recounts the death of Socrates and argues for the immortality of the soul, three or four times. Plutarch recounts this dismissively. Cato is a Stoic, not a true Platonist, like his biographer. He does not embody the living tradition of philosophy, of passing down wisdom from master to student, as Socrates had to Plato. Rather, he is a bookish adherent of a much too cerebral school, and had to read a philosophical instruction manual at least three times before he could plunge into eternity.

146

Melancholia XIII. Ficino is, in his way, a wanderer on a winter's journey, one measured not in footsteps, but in turns of the imagination. In acknowledging that melancholy is both poison and cure, means and ends, he embraces the mind's journey through a bleak winter landscape. And indeed, melancholy is the very condition for any kind of imaginative endeavor, which in turn reveals itself to be the cure for melancholy. In other words, one must seize on the wanderer's drive in order to seize the melancholic drive. It is easier to do this than to say it: while Ficino articulates this through a laborious account of how images relate to planets and the human imagination, Burton makes the theory his own by applying it to himself: he writes about melancholy—an exercise of the mind and imagination—in order to ward off melancholy. Indulge your melancholy, in other words, and see where it leads you. This is where the romantic irony that we first encountered as self-alienation, and that was the poison that runs in the Wanderer's veins, becomes his salvation, *pharmakon* in the full sense. Saturn always brings together opposites; to live in his world is to follow his laws of opposites fading in and out of each other. But if this is to be harnessed as a strength rather than suffered as an intolerable weight, we must approach all things Saturnine with irony, playfulness, and imagination. Just as the *Saturnalia* relieve the unbearable seriousness of the old god on the level of society, so too must the soul approach him with playfulness—seriousness is the downfall of the Saturnine spirit. It is precisely this playfulness, this lightness, that lets one sustain the tension of paradox, and hold opposites together in one's mind. This kind of playfulness uses the energy generated by the coincidence of opposites to produce the wanderer's song, Burton's treatise, Ficino's translations of Plato.

147

I always feel immediately at home when I am back in Tübingen. The brown-rose stone of the University Hall, the colorful half-timbered houses, the inns with their hardwood tables and small green-hued wine glasses—all of it fills with me with the most delicious nostalgia. Only the tower along the river inspires an unshakeable feeling of uncanniness. The tower is at least seven hundred years old. At the beginning of the nineteenth century, it was acquired by one Ernst Friedrich Zimmer. At the same moment, the greatest poet of the nineteenth century, the most astute philosophical mind of his generation and father of dialectic, Friedrich Hölderlin, had been diagnosed as incurably mad. Yet, as if he had diffused his poetic genius in the Swabian atmosphere, lovers of verse intervened on Hölderlin's behalf. At the clinic where he had initially been interned, he was treated by the physician, poet, and esotericist Justinus Kerner. Zimmer, a reader of poetry and admirer of Hölderlin's masterpiece, *Hyperion*, was convinced by the clinic's director to take in the mad poet. Thus begins Hölderlin's tower years, his *Turmzeit*, which would last thirty-six years. If before, he had written obscure, highly philosophical verse, he now wrote with childlike simplicity. And so every time I walk along the banks of the Neckar and see the yellow tower with its tin spire, I am haunted by a doubt: was Hölderlin mad, or was he the sanest of all men?

148

When two of Friedrich Rückert's children died of scarlet fever, his poetic vocation descended with them into the realm of the dead. Rückert would write 428 poems in memory of them. His *Songs on the Death of Children* (*Kindertotenlieder*) is a sustained cry of grief, at once a vast and concentrated expression of mourning. Inspired by ancient oriental poetry, the complaint often takes the form of a ghazal, a song of lost love whose strains were heard even before the Prophet's time. While the theme is always the same—the death of these two children whose universe was restrained in both time and experience—the vastness of Rückert's longing for his dead children is as endless as the desert. Can they really be gone? Death is an eastern kingdom, an opium-nightmare, a red sunset, the fragrance of a gingko tree. It, too, will pass, and cede to something greater: the poet's love. Fascinated by the poems, the composer Gustav Mahler had long intended to set them to music. The theme was too familiar: eight of his siblings had died in childhood. Perhaps for this reason, he hesitated. The project, begun in 1901, would be abandoned for three years. In 1904, two weeks after the birth of his daughter Maria, the composer revisited his *Kindertotenlieder*. This greatly upset his wife Alma. Why tempt fate with such things? Three years later, the child would die of scarlet fever. The music that both announces her death and mourns it evokes the same paradox as Rückert's poetry: concentrated on so small a being and so singular an event, its rich tones and endless melodies cover an immeasurable musical expanse. The listener is at once saddened, consoled, and astounded by this bottomless longing for the irretrievable. Another paradoxical restraint—Mahler only set six of the poems to music. But the two lines with which he begins are the ultimate expression of depth and contrast: "Now the sun wants to rise as brightly/As if there had been no catastrophe in the night."

149

Melancholia XIV. Do you want to know my cure for melancholy? A small dose of mercury. Both quicksilver and god, male and female, a god and a philosophy, Mercurius, or Hermes, is the patron of the alchemist. Mercurius is the psychopomp, the spirit guide, the hurdy-gurdy man at the end of the *Winter's Journey,* but also a joker, a question-asker, a composer of riddles. It is only this trickster-god that can lead you through the paradoxes that old man Saturn presents. So take a dose of this metal that is liquid, learn to be playful and ever-changing, and dive headlong into Saturn's abyss. The old man god is too serious, too engrossed, and lacks the ironic distance necessary to understand human affairs. The quick-silver god would love nothing more than to play a trick on you, and laugh as you misinterpret his words: only the wisest of scholars, grounded by the weight of melancholy thinking, can harness his power. Saturn will teach you to think; Mercurius will teach you not to take yourself seriously. This is the best way to survive a long winter's journey through the night.

150

Now that you have recovered from your bout of melancholy, let me tell you about another disease of the soul, one that can throw you back into melancholy if you do not overcome it: the monomania of the philosophers. What consumption is to poets and madness to hatters, so is this awful affliction the occupational hazard of the speculative thinker. From Parmenides, who thought that all was one, through the idealists of early modernity who conceived of all thinking as a "System," down to the astrophysicist who imposes a "model" on his findings, the desire to arrange everything into a totality—to make all things One—is the theoretical philosopher's stone. It would seem that it is Reason's nature to want to subsume all things under One Principle. Like a broken record, the systematizer has one thing he repeats over and over again, until all other things fade out of memory. But there is always a piece that doesn't fit, and the system-thinker either ceases to see it, or is driven mad by it, overcome by the irrationality whose existence he has refused to acknowledge. What he has forgotten is that Reason stands out from the Irrational like a relief sculpture. Once one realizes this, one sees that the One Principle is a deadweight, the ashes of past struggles of opposites.

151

Lifetimes before he was a scholar, Faust was a blacksmith. Let me tell you this ancient story: A Smith makes a deal with the devil. They signed an agreement: for seven years, he would be the master of his trade. After that, he would belong to the Evil One. When the time had come, the devil appeared at the smithy and said, "come, you will hang yourself on a tall tree. This is the door to my kingdom." The smith took a bag for his head and a rope for his neck, and followed the devil into the forest. Once they had reached a tall elm tree, the smith said, "if I am to hang myself, give me proof that you are who you say you are." The devil answered him, "I am the prince of this world, and I can do all things; I can make myself as great as an elm or as small as a mouse." The blacksmith answered, "we already have an elm. If you are the devil, make yourself into a mouse." And so the devil became a mouse, and the blacksmith caught him and put him in the bag and tied it up with the rope. Then he beat his captive until the devil agreed to give him back the agreement that they had signed so that it could be destroyed. And so the demon limped back to hell, cursing. This fairy tale is one of the oldest stories in human history, as old as language itself. Different versions are told all over the world, with a multitude of variations—sometimes the smith receives power, sometimes gold; sometimes Christ also comes to him, disguised; and the devil is tricked into revoking the agreement in a thousand different ways. In Russia, Germany, and Italy, in Scandinavia, India, and the Basque country, the same tale, more ancient that any one people or language, is told. Indeed, the antiquity of the tale evokes a paradox: the language in which the story was first told, Indo-European, would seem to have no word for "smith." Blacksmithing was the great miracle of the bronze age. Is it a miracle born out of a myth? The blacksmith is greater, but the devil is older.

152

Berlin on a December afternoon. The days are grey, and the sun sets almost before one realizes that it rose. There is more time, then, for the city's denizens to live out the night-passions for which they are famous. One's mind immediately wanders to the height of Berlin decadence, the 1920s. Syphilis-infested brothels, back-alley abortions, secret transvestite clubs, and illicit drugs gave the Berlin night a Dadaist glean. Nothing seemed real, and the night, infinite and dream-like, opened simultaneously its stores of both pleasure and horror. Some black and white photographs, found in a box in an abandoned corner of a second-hand shop in Prenzlauer Berg, offer a kaleidoscope view of Weimar decadence. We find, going through them in no particular order: three elephants, led by their Indian masters, walk solemnly through the Tiergarten; two prostitutes buy small sachets of cocaine on a street-corner; two bare-chested men in rouge, wearing naval officers' hats, dance at a transvestite ball; Marlene Dietrich, dressed in tails and top hat, appears on stage, stony-faced. These remind me of Berlin as I first knew it, in the 1990s, when the same mood prevailed. The former factories of the former East-Berlin became nightclubs. Before the whole world flocked to them, these places, some of them consecrated exclusively to homosexual pleasures in near-total darkness (and perfect anonymity), were places in which all things seemed possible, and the sun never rose—one could walk into Berghain on Friday night and emerge, bleary-eyed and defeated, on Monday afternoon. This account, however, is only second hand. In those days, I went to bed early, and besides, I never liked Berlin. It is a city with too much night.

153

Why is there something rather than nothing? Who first asked this question? Leibniz? Augustine? It is the sort of question that may be as old as language itself. As soon as we begin to speak, it draws us in—we talk about our world, and wonder *why*. But I would not recommend that you be drawn into this question. If it has any worth, it is in showing the limits of our questioning, of what it means to ask questions at all. *Why* is the refrain of the rational force within you, the daytime reflex of confronting the world by taking it apart, analyzing it piece by piece, and then putting it back together again as a rational construct. *Why* is the great tool of rational understanding, a little word that magically transforms things; what was simply present before—a gingko tree, a piece of quartz, a ruined pillar—must now be taken apart and violently interrogated. The interrogation is infinite, with an endless series of inquisitors taking turns: biologists, historians, anthropologists, and worst of all, philosophers conspire to wear the object down until it has been atomized. And even once the world has been broken down into a swarm of atoms—the basic building blocks of chemistry, biology, linguistics, and meaning itself—the incessant questioning of rationality does not stop. Never satisfied, reason continues to take things apart, searching for the origins of all things, the beginning of everything. The only thing that can escape this atomizing force is *will*. Only a will, a power of volition, can resist objectification. There is perhaps some wisdom, then, in the myths of creation that tell of a god who makes the world of things, willing it into existence. If there is an ultimate, satisfactory answer to the question *why*, then it must lie in the power of will. But this is not a happy resolution: embodied by the word *why*, the force of reason then wrestles with the creative will. It cannot help itself, it must ask *why* this First Will created the world in the first place. But the Will resists, and retreats into itself. Moreover, the continued questioning of reason pushes all that it cannot recognize, all that is irrational, into the realm of pure willing. The First Will, filled with all that is irrational and dark, therefore rears its head and pushes back: the questioner now finds himself rationalizing an evil and irrational universe in the same way a sailor stands dry on the deck of his ship while bounded by the ocean. *Why* is therefore not only an unproductive question, but an unhappy one. The rational mind, the day-thinker, must therefore find a way of dealing with what is Other, what is new, what is not one's own thoughts, in a less abstract way. The atomizing force of reason must be hemmed in by the whole. Day must come out night. A better question for reason, then, would be: *how do I open myself up to something radically new?*

154

What happens, then, when night and day, light and darkness, reason and simply being-there, cooperate, and find a shared center? To speak in naïve terms: the Good. Evil, then, would not be some sort of privation of the good, but a misalignment of things, a move away from the productive center point where things are balanced. Day, paradoxically, is a destructive force: in order to build up, it must first take apart in order to analyze and understand. Night would then be a healing force, a time not only of darkness and privation, but also for sleep and restoration, when the whole is reconstituted after the atomizing violence of the day. Look for evil on white nights and moonlit days. It is no lack, but rather a perversion: when the forces that keep things in balance, night and day, go out of joint, evil ensues. What is truly evil is parasitic on the good, but ultimately unfruitful in itself—it cannot feed itself, but must always draw its sustenance from what is Good. Can there be a sunless day if dawn has become completely unimaginable? If the twin promises of dawn and dusk become unimaginable, then all things simply pass away.

155

Breath-taking. Not syphilis, madness, or addiction but, instead, tuberculosis has robbed us of more writers than any other affliction. And while today, it is treated with antibiotics, until the middle of the twentieth century, it was the White Plague. This malady that robbed one of breath seemed, paradoxically, to be an affliction of poets. For romantic medicine, it was a problem of combustion: the lungs, the engine of the body, could not take in enough air to fuel the machine. The organism therefore *consumed* itself, and those who suffered from consumption grew thin and wasted away. The poet, who pours his entire soul into a few dense lines, makes himself vulnerable to the disease through his excitable imagination. He works into the night, writing verses, taking stimulants to stay alert, whittling down the very stuff of his existence into verse. Here, writes Keats (who succumbed to the disease aged twenty-five) is "where youth grows pale, and spectre-thin, and dies." The only cure is a total cessation of literary activity. The expenditure of verses must be paid back in kind, with silence and rest. It is not a solution that the poet, whose vocation is to create, can readily accept. Hence the poets fall one after another: Keats and Novalis, Brontë and Browning, Chekhov and Kafka. Others are confined to sanatoriums, living a horizontal life of forced contemplation. And what is left of this cure when the world itself has been romanticized, liable to be consumptive? In imagination, we are co-authors of the world itself, constantly exerting our spiritual faculties. The *Sehnsucht* or yearning of the beautiful soul cannot be consummated, and so it consumes itself. Hegel's diagnosis is judicious: "The beautiful soul, lacking all actuality, caught in the contradiction between its pure self and its necessity to empty itself into being and to turn itself around into actuality," is thus "shattered into madness and melts into a yearning, tubercular consumption." Even after Hegel has broken its spell, there is a romantic aftershock, an existentialist consumption that stands feverishly on the threshold of nihilism. This kind of consumption, which is everywhere in Dostoyevsky (Raskolnikov and Kateryna in *Crime and Punishment*, Hippolit in *The Idiot*) will be acted out by the likes of Camus and Deleuze. Roland Barthes lives out Mann's *Magic Mountain*, and then spends his post-penicillin life leading a sanatorium-inspired contemplative existence. The dissolution of the romantic-consumptive myth that comes with broad access to penicillin is a process that stands at the threshold between spirit and matter, medicine and myth. The Hegelian decree descends upon the laboratory—and then back out of it, into a new realm of meaning.

156

La béance. Literally, the word means "gap" or "opening." But its most frequent utterers, psychoanalysts, use it to refer to a distance that cannot be traversed, a desire that cannot be fulfilled. If animals go from one fulfilment to another, we, the beings capable of overthinking, of endless rumination, are never really satisfied. The *béance* is ultimately a nostalgia for the absolute, a longing for the whole, where our desire would find satisfaction. We carry this inextinguishable desire like a wound, a mark, placed on us like the one that God placed upon Cain after he murdered his brother. It is the mark of sorrow, but also the source of hope.

157

Imaginary Libraries. In no particular order, some ancient books that are lost to history: the *Margites,* a comic epic ascribed to Homer; two treatises of Thales, *On the Equinox,* and *On the Solstice*; thirty-five plays by Aeschylus, lost either in whole or part; thirty-eight plays by Sophocles, lost either in whole or part; everything that Socrates may (or may not) have written; virtually all of Aristotle's treatises and dialogues—only a third of his writings have survived, most of them lecture notes never meant to be shared; four mathematical treatises by Euclid, and two by Archimedes; a seven-book history of Rome by Cato the Elder; the Egyptian book of Thoth.

158

Because Orpheus descended into hell and returned, he was viewed by some as a god, and became the object of a mysterious religion, the Orphic cult. Its adepts revered all those who had returned from hell: Persephone, who made the journey to the underworld annually, and Dionysius, who had died and been reborn, and who was prophesied to do it again—the third Dionysius is the mysterious god of the future. Indeed, it is this myth of the god of the future that Orpheus brings back from the underworld, his own rite of passage in following the secret ways of Dionysius. In order to achieve immortality as a spiritual being, one had to be initiated into the mysteries of Dionysius, undergoing ritual purification. Otherwise, one would be condemned to the way of Persephone, descending and reascending from the dead, being indefinitely reincarnated as a material being. More than any other religion of antiquity, Orphism was about a future that we anticipate, but cannot foretell: who knows what the god will bring out of the darkness of the underworld?

159

My guide in Amsterdam was W***, perhaps the greatest living scholar of esoteric philosophy. Under the cover of narrow side-streets and tree-lined canals, he spoked in hushed tones as he led me to a secret destination. The *Sefer Raziel Hamalakh*, he said, the *Book of the Angel Raziel*, is one of the most incredible kabbalistic texts. Purportedly given by the angel Raziel to Adam, it contains a number of spells, a method for writing protective amulets, and an elaborate numerology. In Renaissance Germany, it was considered the summit of magical texts, at times praised by saints as a mystical treatise, at others decried as a vile work of necromancy. As we entered the complex of the Portuguese synagogue, W*** told me that he would show me a rare gem: a medieval Hebrew-Aramaic copy of the text. In the Ets Haim library, which contains the most extensive collection of kabbalistic texts outside of Israel, and to which W*** has unlimited access, we searched for hours. W*** insisted that he had seen it many times before, and that he had never had any trouble finding it. An old man wearing a kippah, slight of build and diminutive in stature, watched us from behind an enormous desk piled with ancient tomes. It is certainly here, he told us. You just have to be determined enough to find it.

160

Adrian Leverkühn sits at the piano. The notes he plays make no sense to his listener. Their terrible dissonances have left melody and tone behind. It is devil's music, and when his listener—an old companion from his school days—comments on its uncanny effect, Leverkühn answers, "You will remember that during our philosophy studies we learned that to impose a limit is already to overstep it." With these words, the musician reminds the philosopher of a lesson that is easily forgotten. The advancement of knowledge is a quest for infinite light. How long before one is blinded by its brightness? Those who have reached the summit and gone blind have learned the lesson the hard way. Seeing and seen should not be confused, and there is more to vision than what appears. The fullness of seeing and the triumph of light, the element in which seeing bathes, implies the destruction of all things. One could also say the same with a mythological flourish: no one can see God and live. Perception, then, is always a matter of restraint. We see only small figures against a vast sky, and must hold on to these things lest we be annihilated. Wisdom is light, but recognizing it requires some shadow. We are chiaroscuro beings, thinkers of the sunset. Or to return to Leverkühn's musical-philosophical idiom, our finitude is not a limit, but precisely the sign of our capacity for transcendence. Recall that *in-finite* is a negation—not the fullness of something at first incomplete, but merely the negation of the starting point. But to see this, we must free ourselves from our obsession with Oneness, and consign part of what we are to shadow.

161

Ours is an age of pathologizing, and some venerable white-coated figure might try (or maybe has already succeeded) in persuading you that your night is a disease. The real disease, however, is to forget that the day came out of the night, and that you must continue to hold your night in you. The sun sets and rises again; your rational thoughts, necessary for your existence, are painted on the canvass of a dream. Let's repeat in white-coat jargon: you cannot be reduced to your desires. Rather, there is a desiring self that stands behind the desiring. This provides the matrix for all being, always a unity of the twofold. The world is shot through with this duality: the real and the ideal, conscious and unconscious, self and other. In order to open oneself up to something new, one must split the self off from the core of one's being, and this is the very movement of desire. Desire is therefore necessarily and *productively* dissociative. Our wholeness lies not in the past, but in the future, the object of constant striving. The classic theory of *repression* follows this model. Some intolerable corner reality, the place where my desires are thwarted, is thrust into the night, and no longer speaks to me in daytime words. And perhaps this is so. But the dissociative is not merely the repressed. If it were so, our whole élan of desires would be turned towards the past—Thanatos would have won out over eros. No, desire moves us forward, beyond ourselves, and seen from the night, the day is not enemy, but ecstasy.

162

Perchance to dream VIII. After having been lost for nearly a century, Emanuel Swedenborg's dream diary was rediscovered in the Swedish National Library, and finally published in 1859. The *Drömboken* begins on July 21st, 1743 as the fifty-five-year-old sage is on his way to the Netherlands. It ends on October 26–27 of 1744, with Swedenborg beginning the composition of his book *De cultu et amore dei*. The *Dream Book* is a feast of visions. Part travel diary, it chronicles a journey that begins in Stockholm, the city of its author's birth, to Straslund, Hamburg, Bremen, Groningen, and finally the Hague, where the majority of the dreams will be written. He sees fortresses, churches, monasteries, ruins, grand hotels, ships and stormy seas. For an eighteenth century man, this would have been a magnificent visual spectacle. It is matched by a spiritual one: the world of dreams captured by an inner vision, the fantastic, disturbing, exalting sights of the dream world. So it is with Swedenborg, who is an unequalled spiritual painter—one eye on the world of bodies, the other on the world of spirits. As his two eyes come in and out of focus, the two landscapes merge, separate, and blur. As we move abruptly from travel diary to dream diary in the first pages, we read a list of places about which our Seer has dreamt: Venice, Sweden, Leipzig. Two kinds of place, spiritual and physical, are intertwined. So are two kinds of man—one who loves himself, and one who loves only God. But soon, they will break apart. Shortly after arriving in the Hague, he dreams that he was "reclining on a mountain beneath which there was an abyss." He is without a foothold, trying to escape the abyss below. Perhaps the body cannot follow the spirit up the mountain, and is liable to fall into the abyss; perhaps he is resisting the power of God, which draws the spirit upwards. The abyss would seem to be what separates the two kinds of men, and the kinds of vision, both of which belong to our Seer. A few nights later, they are bound together again: the dreamer becomes intertwined in a moving machine like a foetus in the womb. A series of abyssal dreams follows, an attempt to bridge the unbridgeable: stairways, holes, and ladders appear; a man is transformed into a woman (could this be anything other than Hermes, the changeling messenger god?); a carriage is driven into water. This unbearable tension of opposites reaches a frenzy. At Easter, Swedenborg believes he is damned. God brings him consolation, and the "temptation" of thinking himself consigned to eternal flames subsides. This relief does not last, however, and the whole process repeats, with the Seer again working himself into a frenzied state. Like a sonata, the themes repeat until a coda is reached. In October 1744, he dreams of a great King and Queen—The Lord God and *Sophia*, Lady Wisdom. They are sovereign, magnanimous, glorious, wanting for nothing. He intuits that he will embark on a great work. In another dream, the sitting-room in his lodgings (now in London) has been transformed into a market-place, full of porcelain vessels. The gaping abyss is now a beautiful incubator, ready to contain an offering. When he awoke, there came upon him "such a swoon or fainting fit as I had experienced six or seven years ago in Amsterdam, when I entered upon the *Oeconomia Regni Animalis,* but it was much more subtle, so that I seemed near to death... This signifies, as at the former time, that my head is being put in order." Here the dream diary ends. Swedenborg goes from being mere Seer to Witness, and begins writing *De cultu et amore dei.* It is not that Swedenborg dreamt this book into being. Rather, the sensuous external experience of travel and the imaginative inner experience of the dreams produced a friction, a productive tension from which the book arose. Most readers of the *Dream Diary* would assume that the dreams were a kind of *catharsis* that cleared the way for writing. It is the opposite: living and dreaming stood in tension, and it is writing that released it. Once dreaming and living have exhausted each other, the remainder is the book.

163

In Paris, again. I will confess to you that I do not like it here. I tolerate the grey Hausmannian buildings, those forefathers of brutalist blocks, and I put up with the noise that penetrates into them from the filthy boulevards. All of this is cushioned by a compulsive routine that sees me spending the daylight hours shut up in reading rooms or caught between shelves, rue Richelieu or Quai François Mauriac. My Parisian book hunts overexcite my fragile psyche and worsen my insomnia, and this city of too-bright night-time lights usually brings on a case of nervous exhaustion. But that is of no importance. I am looking for something: a little notebook bound in parchment, its title only *1 January 1619*. It has been missing since the end of the seventeenth century, but I do not believe it is gone forever. No, there are too many books in this labyrinthine city with its labyrinthine libraries that have gone missing for a few centuries and then suddenly reappeared. One wonders if it is not a question of the book *wanting to be found*. And this little book, I am convinced, is calling out to me, reaching out beyond its little nook, appearing to me in dreams and reveries, repeating to me the fragmentary things I already know about it: that it is called the *Olympica*; that its first six pages are blank; that it contains a number of pages of mathematical formulas and meditations, written upside-down; and that twelve pages in Latin contain René Descartes's account of the three most important dreams of his life.

164

Dreamt but real, lost but not lost, the little parchment book was found among Descartes papers when he died in Stockholm in 1650. Hector-Pierre Chanut, French ambassador to Sweden and friend of the philosopher, took it upon himself to penetrate the drafty rooms where his countryman had succumbed to pleurisy, and make a catalogue of the papers in Descartes's strongboxes. Chanut's catalogue contains twenty-three items, among them the little parchment book dating from 1619, and which contains the marginal note "11 November 1620. I began to understand the marvelous discovery." Chanut sent the chests to his brother-in-law, a printer and man of letters, Claude Clerselier. It was most likely while the papers were in Clerselier's possession that a certain Monsieur Godefroy Leibnitz, a young man of learning come from Hannover, examined the *Olympica* and read Descartes's dreams. In his own little notebook, the *Cogitationes Privatae* (which was itself lost for a number of centuries until it, too, wanted to be found), Leibniz remarks that Descartes was an esotericist and Rosicrucian, his dreams and private writings full of symbols dear to the adepts of the Rosy Cross. The next we hear of the Olympica is in Abbé Baillet's 1691 biography, *La vie de Monsieur Des Cartes*. He sometimes translates and sometimes paraphrases the twelve pages of dream-stuff, their content taken up into his Cartesian mythology. In any event, he is the last known reader of the *Olympica*, and our source for the dreams.

But I am sure it is here somewhere, in some neglected corner, hidden in the creases of a folio, down in the basement of the *Collection de l'enfer*—a lovely chamber of curiosities both pornographic and esoteric that I have never been allowed to visit...

165

November 1619. After witnessing the coronation of Emperor Ferdinand II, Descartes went to the Bavarian countryside. Cut off from the world, he spent his days in a room with a little stove ("Il demeuroit tout le jour enfermé feul dans un poêfle"), and thought. Enraptured in thought, enveloped in it, Descartes's thinking was no less rigorous for having becoming a meditative practice. One wonders if this protracted contemplative state, this fit of thinking, was not some tubercular hallucination, a brain-fever that excited the imagination. Little wonder these were feverish days: Descartes was cooking his mind in his little stove, performing an alchemical nigredo, boiling all his thoughts down to a black paste. And through this impossible transformation, this painful breaking down of the old mind, a new kind of contemplation emerged, a modern way of attending to oneself that stands alongside Pascal's *Pensées* and Ignatius's *Exercises*: the *Meditations*. This alchemy of the mind led him to spend hours entertaining fantasies about the architecture of thought, the building up and tearing down of mental cities. Like a squalid neighborhood that must be demolished and rebuilt in uniform style, the constructions of the mind—up until now chaotic, ugly, insalubrious— would have to be cast down, and the mental city rebuilt according to Reason's plan. And so he would tear everything down first, and destroy the *doxa* in himself. Did he understand the violence of this gesture? The agitation it produced culminated in three intense dreams, all dreamt on 10 November, Saint Martin's night, as the rest of the town was in revelry.

166

The three dreams of Monsieur Descartes.

Apeliotes. The dreamer is walking through the streets of a city, terrorized by ghosts. The fear they provoked was such that he was struck by a kind of apoplexy, and his right side became weak. Lame and hunched over, he is now hit by a strong and unrelenting wind that further hinders his movements. He sees a college in the distance, and decides to take refuge in its chapel. On the way, he passes an acquaintance, and turning to greet the man, who had not seen him, he was again rebuffed by the terrible wind. In the College yard stood another acquaintance. The man called out to the dreamer by name and said, "Monsieur N. has something for you." The dreamer imagined that it must be a melon from some faraway land. After calling out to him, the man continued to talk with those around him, all of whom stood up straight, unperturbed by the terrible wind. Descartes awoke fearing that some evil genie had possessed him, and with pain in his left side. He turned over onto his right side and lay there for two hours, thinking, before falling back asleep.

Jupiter. The dreamer hears a loud crack that he takes to be thunder, and he awakes with a start. Opening his eyes, he sees that the room is filled with sparks that dance about in the darkness. Through opening and closing his eyes, and then focusing on the objects visible to him through the obscurity, he is able to calm himself until the sparks pass. He then falls into a peaceful sleep.

Hamlet. The dreamer finds a book of unknown origin lying on his table. Upon opening it, he discovers that it is a dictionary, something that pleases him immensely—he could make good use of one. Suddenly, a second book appears, a collection of poetry called *Corpus Poëtarum &c.* He opens it to a random page, and his eyes fall upon the lines *Quod vitae sectabor iter,* what path in life will I pursue? As he sits at his table with his books, a man appears before him, and starts to recite some verses that begin with *Est & non...,* yes and no. The dreamer finds them very good, and congratulating the player, says to him, "I know these verses well. They are from the *Idyls of Ausone,* and are found here in this anthology I have before me." The player asks where the book came from, and the dreamer says that he does not know. It appeared to him with another book—but where has it gone? The dictionary has moved from one end of the table to another, and does not look the same. In the meantime, our dreamer has found the Idyls he was looking for in the anthology. But he could not find the piece that began with *Yes and no.* "But I know another by the same author that is more beautiful," says the dreamer, "one that begins with the words *What path in life will I pursue.*" As he looks for it, he finds some pages with engravings that make him think that this book is very beautiful. As his admiration for it grew, his familiarity with its contents faded, and he could not find the poem from earlier. The dreamscape then changes, with books and interlocutor suddenly disappearing.

167

Lectiones hermeticae. Monsieur Baillet then tells us how Descartes interpreted his dreams. But I do not believe him. This, I am sure, is a fabrication on the part of the historian, and I have my reasons for this, as you will soon find out. Once I find the little parchment book, it will be clear that there is no interpretation of the dreams, or at least not what Baillet recounts. And perhaps some of the most fantastic dream imagery was excised to fit the narrative. Don't all editors do that? Who knows how badly redacted these lines will be by the time they reach you, dream reader. But we should finish Baillet's account: Still not awake—or in some state between sleeping and dreaming—Descartes says to himself, this must have been a dream. The dictionary must have been the symbol of all the sciences brought together; the anthology of poetry, wisdom and philosophy: for even the most frivolous of poets can speak wisdom, given by grace of divine *enthusiasm* (that is, inspiration) and imagination, which dance in the mind like sparks. The verse *What path...* represents good council. Descartes then wakes up, and continues to interpret his dream: the poets represent divine revelation and enthusiasm; the *Est & non*, the yes and no of Pythagoras, is the difference between truth and falseness in the sciences. Indeed, it would seem that it was the spirit of truth that sent him this dream, opening up all the treasures of the sciences to him. And this third dream signified the future, while the other two, his sinful past. The melon he was offered in the first dream represented "the charms of solitude, but solicited solely through human and not divine means." The ill wind was an evil genie who was pushing him forcefully to a place where he ought to voluntarily go. The clap of thunder in the second dream was the spirit of truth descending upon him. One element remained that bothered him: what were the engravings? Two days later, an Italian painter came to visit him, meaning that they must have been an omen. Descartes will busy himself with these dreams and their meaning for his vocation for a few more days, but soon, his feverish mental state passes, and he turns towards the intellectual projects with which he will busy himself that winter.

168

I dream before I am. Are we to take this to mean that the father of rationalism received his method in a dream? In the *Meditations*, the vividness of dreams casts doubt on the senses' ability to know the truth. Have we not all had dreams that we thought were real? And what if some evil genius sent not only ill winds, but vivid dreams, and constructed a whole dream-world in which we live and cannot escape? What prevents this from being the case? Only the goodness of God and the clearness and distinctness of ideas—that is, the foundations of science that come from God, the most fundamental of which is this: *I think, therefore I am.* But if the foundations of sciences were given in a dream, a gift from God, what becomes of Descartes's system? This was Baillet's fear, the reason for all the tampering I suspect. According to the story we have heard, the dreams do not contain "Science." They do not even announce it. They begin coming into language as Descartes begins coming to consciousness, gradually, each element finding its place. Indeed, Baillet's account is one in which Descartes is constructing a dream-system that forces him to step into the truth and embark upon the path of science. It is only once the dreams are left behind and the words in which they are interpreted take their place that science begins; it is only when he steps out of the overheated room that his work commences. Descartes is not so much interpreting his dreams as he is incorporating his life into a dream-narrative: Saint Martin's night, the stove, the little house, the frenzy of solitude, the fire that excited his brain—these are all indispensable elements of the dream. So while it is clear that Baillet has worked hard to separate Descartes's dreams from Descartes's science, the two inevitably collide. It is no wonder that Leibniz, who saw the original text, thinks M. Baillet misinterprets what Descartes means by "science." Leibniz thought that Descartes meant secret, gnostic knowledge, the knowledge that only comes in dreams. But Leibniz would seem to misunderstand the relationships of these two spheres as well. When Descartes will recount the beginnings of his attempt at a *tabula rasa* of all science in the *Discourse on Method*, he will only mention being shut up in a little stove-heated room, alone with his thoughts. The dreams, it would seem, are the houses that must be demolished before science can be built up. They are not the by-products of his imagination. Rather *Science* is the by-product, the *caput mortuum* of the dream: the only thing that does not fit into Descartes dream-world is what it announces: the *Cogito*.

169

Melon, Engraving. A thought experiment: It is 1929, you are a Frenchman named Maxime Leroy, and you are writing a book about René Descartes. Imagine also that you are both perplexed by the three dreams from Saint Martin's night in 1619, and mistrustful of Baillet's account of them. And so you write to the Viennese *Traummeister*, Sigmund Freud, hoping he will be able to verify some hypotheses of yours. Of course, you would, under those circumstances, offer your own paraphrase of Baillet's text—like some Delphic oracle, you get out of Freud what you put into Freud. But the father of psychoanalysis is used to people lying to him about dreams, and he is in any case much cleverer than you. And so he goes to the Viennese National Library, where almost anything can be found (indeed, it is my next stop on this wild goose-chase), and reads Baillet for himself. And then he sends you the most revealing non-answer in the history of dream interpretation. In a curt letter of a page and a half, Freud tells Leroy that there is no dream without the dreamer, and it is only the dreamer of the dream who can interpret it. All the more with these particular dreams, which are *Träume von Oben*. These dreams from above are intellectual ones, formulations of ideas that could have been made during the day. This kind of dream is therefore a hieroglyph, and only the dreamer can explain what it means. And Descartes (or at least Baillet) does indeed explain the dreams. But not all of it—and here is where the Unconcious comes into play:

the elements missing from the dreamer's explanation are the real content of the unconscious. Here, writes Freud, there are two elements whose explanation is adequate: the melon and the engravings. They are also the two most bizarre elements, the ones that Descartes would rather avoid. Freud muses on the melon (the sexual fantasies that came to him in solitude—forbidden fruit?), but says nothing about the engravings. Freud says no more on the matter, and even withholds an important piece of information: nothing is ever really absurd in a dream, even if in the context of a "dream from above," some elements do not fit. The world of dreaming and the world in which its interpretation takes place are two different systems, two spheres that can overlap, but never fully coincide. And precisely the most absurd element for the waking system may be the most meaningful for the dream system.

PHILOSOPHICAL FRAGMENTS

Crieur de Melons (Melon Peddler), 1690–91
Engraving
Bibliothèque nationale de France

170

Ode to the Night

You darkness out of which I came
I love you much more than the flame,
World-confining,
Only shining
In that restricted sphere,
Beyond which nothing bright could still adhere.

But darkness gathers all into its heart:
Forms and flames, beasts and art
All as they are,
And men and might—

So near and yet so far
A power stirs, a tutelary star.

My faith is in the Night.

—Rainer Maria Rilke

NOTES

Preface

Gott spricht zu jedem nur, ...; Rainer Maria Rilke, *Das Stunden-Buch*, 3 vols. (Leipzig: Insel-Verlag, 1905), 1:59.

Vita brevis, ars longa; it is not a Latin phrase at all, but from the opening paragraph of the *Corpus Hippocraticum* (1.1): Ὁ βίος βραχὺς, ἡ δὲ τέχνη μακρὴ. Hippocrates is not concerned with "art" as we usually understand it, but rather with "techné."

"Darkness and concealment..."; F.W.J. Schelling, *The Ages of the World* (1811), translated and with an introduction by Joseph P. Lawrence (SUNY Press, 2019), 83.

Frag. 2

I remember thee upon my bed; Psalm 63:6 (KJV)

Frag. 5

More geometrico; according to the methods of geometry. Cf. Spinoza's 1663 work in two parts on Descartes's philosophical principles, *Renati des Cartes Principiorum Philosophae*, which is subtitled *More Geometrico demonstratæ*.

Frag. 9

To die—to sleep, ...; William Shakespeare, *Hamlet*, 3.1.

Frag. 10

Ennui; Charles Baudelaire, "Au Lecteur," in *Les Fleurs du Mal*, Édition de 1861 (Gallimard, 1972), 34.

Frag. 11

"The Uncanny" [1919], in *The Standard Edition of the Complete Psychological Works of Sigmund Freud*, translated by James Strachey, 24 vols. (The Hogarth Press, and the Institute of Psycho-Analysis 1953–74), 17: 218–52.

Frag. 13

"attente/waiting," in Roland Barthes, *A Lover's Discourse: Fragments*, translated by Richard Howard (Hill and Wang, 1978), 37–40.

Frag. 14

"Upon my flowering breast..."; *The Collected Works of St. John of the Cross*, translated by Kieran Kavanaugh and Otilio Rodriguez (ICS Publications/Institute of Carmelite Studies, 1979), 296.

"As long as I see your eyes open..."; Johann Wolfgang Goethe, *Die Leiden des jungen Werther* (Insel Verlag, 2006), 38 (Letter of 19 June; my translation).

Frag. 15

Sigmund Freud, "Beyond the Pleasure Principle" [1920], in *The Standard Edition*, 1: 57.

Frag. 18

"As virtuous men pass..."; John Donne, "A Valediction: Forbidding Mourning," *www.poetryfoundation.org/poems/44131/a-valediction-forbidding-mourning*.

Frag. 20

"In time the curtain-edges will grow light..."; Philip Larkin, "Aubade," *www.poetryfoundation.org/poems/48422/aubade-56d229a6e2f07*.

Marcel Proust, *Swann's Way* [1913], translated by Lydia Davis (Penguin Books, 2004).

Frag. 21

Aristotle, *Problemata* 30.1 (954a11–1498), in *The Complete Works of Aristotle*, 2 vols., edited by Jonathan Barnes (Princeton University Press, 1991), 2: 1500ff.

Raymond Klibansky, Erwin Panofsky, and Franz Saxl, *Saturn and Melancholy: Studies in the History of Natural Philosophy, Religion, and Art* [1964] (McGill-Queen's University Press, 2019), 15–16.

Frag. 31

Why, then, all this pain and yearning?... ; Goethe, *The Wanderer's Nightsong I.*

Frag. 34

taedium sive anxietatem cordis; Jean Cassien, *Institutions cénobitiques* 10.1 (Les Éditions du Cerf, 2001), 384–85.

Frag. 35

Karl Jaspers, "Diurnal Law and Noctural Passion," in *Philosophy*, vol. 3: *Metaphysics* [1932], translated by E.B. Ashton (The University of Chicago Press, 1971), 95.

E.M. Cioran, *The Trouble with Being Born* [1973], translated by Richard Howard (Arcade Publishing, 1976), 85.

Frag. 37

Anonymous [Valentin Tomberg], *Meditations on the Tarot: A Journey into Christian Hermeticism*, translated by Robert A. Powell (Amity House, 1985), Letter 1: The Magician.

Frag. 38

Aristotle, *Metaphysics*, translated by W.D. Ross (Clarendon Press, 1908), Book II.

Frag. 39

Angelo Maria Ripellino, *Magic Prague* [1973], translated by David Newton Marinelli; edited by Michael Henry Heim (University of California Press, 1994), 62.

Frag. 40

Divertissement; Blaise Pascal, *Œuvres complètes*, 2 vols. (Gallimard, 2000), 2: 583 [*Pensée* 126].

Frag. 41

Rainer Maria Rilke, *The Notebooks of Malte Laurids Brigge,* [1910], translated by Stephen Mitchell (Vintage Books, 1990), 103-4.

Manfred Engel, "'Weder Seiende, noch Schauspieler': Zum Subjektivitätsentwurf in Rilkes 'Malte Laurids Brigge,'" in *Rilke Heute: Der Ort des Dichters in der Moderne,* edited by Vera Hauschild (Suhrkamp Verlag, 1997), 181-200.

Frag. 44

Robert Burton, *The Anatomy of Melancholy,* edited by Angus Gowland (Penguin Classics, 2021).

László F. Földényi, *Melancholy* [1984], translated by Tim Wilkinson (Yale University Press, 2016), 4.

Frag. 47

Dante Alighieri, *Inferno,* Canto 27. Montefeltro's remark about not wanting to confide in the living is used as the epigraph to T. S. Eliot's "The Lovesong of J. Alfred Prufrock"; *www.poetryfoundation.org/poetrymagazine/poems/44212/the-love-song-of-j-alfred-prufrock.*

Frag. 53

A General Collection of Discourses of the Virtuosi of France, Upon Questions of All Sorts of Philosophy, and Other Natural Knowledge Made in the Assembly of the Beaux Esprits *at* Paris, *by the Most Ingenious Persons of that Nation Render'd into English by G. Havers, Gent* (London, 1664), ch. 33.1: Of Those That Walk in Their Sleep.

Frag. 64

Emmanuel Levinas, *Time and the Other* [1979], translated by Richard A. Cohen (Duquesne University Press, 1987), 49ff.

Frag. 71

Henry Chapman, *Iconoclasm and Later Prehistory* (Routledge, 2018).

David M. Gwynn, "From Iconoclasm to Arianism: The Construction of Christian Tradition in the Iconoclast Controversy," *Greek, Roman, and Byzantine Studies* 47 (2007): 225-51.

Alain Besançon, *L'Image interdite: Une histoire intellectuelle de l'iconoclasme* (Fayard, 1994).

Frag. 73

E.H. Gombrich, *Symbolic Images: Studies in the Art of the Renaissance* (Phaidon, 1975), 102ff. ("Hypnerotomachiana").

Frag. 75

1 Samuel 3: 1–15

Frag. 79

Goethe, *Faust: Der Tragödie erster Teil* ("Auerbachs Keller in Leipzig").

Frag. 80

Aristotle, *Metaphysics* 1029b13-14.

Frag. 82

Földényi, *Melancholy*, 29-30.

Frag. 83

Maurice Blanchot, *L'espace littéraire* (Gallimard, 1955), 17ff.

Frag. 84

Emmanuel Levinas, *Existence and Existents* [1963], translated by Alphonso Lingis (Kluwer Academic Publishers, 1978), 65ff.

Frag. 90

Sigmund Freud, *The Interpretation of Dreams* [1899], in *The Standard Edition*, 4: 463–64.

Frag. 91

Jorge Luis Borges, *Ficciones* [1944], translated by Anthony Kerrigan (Grove Weidenfeld, 1962).

Frag. 92

Levinas, *Existence and Existents*, 62ff.

Frag. 93

Friedrich Nietzsche, *The Gay Science* [1882], translated by Josefine Nauckhoff and Adrian del Caro (Cambridge University Press, 2001), par. 341.

Frag. 94

John 3:1–15

Frag. 95

Ovid, *The Metamorphosis*, translated by David Raeburn (Penguin Books, 2004), Book 11.

Frag. 98

The Oldest Systematic Program of German Idealism [1797].

Wolfram Hogrebe, *Predication and Genesis: Metaphysics as Fundamental Heuristic after Schelling's* The Ages of the World [1989], translated and edited by Iain Hamilton Grant and Jason M. Wirth (Edinburgh University Press, 2024).

Frag. 99

See Peter-Klaus Schuster's two-volume account of the various interpretations of it in *Melencholia I: Dürers Denkbild* (Gebr. Mann Verlag, 1991).

Frag. 102

David T. M. Frankfurter, "Stylites and Phallobates: Pillar Religions in Late Antique Syria," *Vigilae Christianae* 44, no. 2 (1990): 168–98.

S. Ashbrook Harvey, "The Sense of a Stylite: Perspectives on Symeon the Elder," *Vigiliae Christianae* 42, no. 44 (1988): 376–94.

Frag. 103

Blanchot, *L'espace littéraire*, 279.

Frag. 104

Ovid, *Metamorphoses*, Book X; cf. C. W. Gluck, *Orfeo et Eurydice* [1762], French libretto by Pierre-Louis Moline [1774].

Frag. 105

Wolfram Hogrebe, *Predication and Genesis*, 74.

Frag. 106

Marguerite Yourcenar, *The Abyss* [*L'oeuvre au noir*, 1968] (Farrar, Strauss and Giroux, 1976).

"S'abîmer/To be engulfed," in Barthes, *A Lover's Discourse*.

"Psychologia vera, oder Viertzig Fragen von der Seelen" [1620], in Jacob Boehme, *Sämtliche Schriften*, edited by Will-Erich Peuckert, vol. 3 (Frommann-Holzboog, 1960).

Frag. 107

"The deep well knows..."; Hugo von Hofmannsthal, "Weltgeheimnis" ["Der tiefe Brunnen weiß es wohl..." [1894]; my translation.

Frag. 114

Rainer Maria Rilke, *Letters to a Young Poet* [1929], translated by M.D. Herter Norton (W.W. Norton, 1954), 59.

Frag. 115

Novalis, "Hymnen an die Nacht"; "Blüthenstaub," in *Schriften: Die Werke Friedrich von Hardenbergs*, edited by Paul Kluckhorn and Richard Samuel (W. Kohlhammer, 1960–).

Frag. 120

Plato, *Meno* 82*b*–84*c*; *Phaedo* 72*e*–77*a*.

Dante, *Purgatorio*, Canto 33, lines 91–99.

Frag. 125

Chaim Vital (1542–1620), *Sefer Etz Chaim* (MSS, from 1572ff.; first print, Korets, 1782).

Sefer ha-Derushim (MS: 1620; print: Yeshivat Ahavat Shalom, 1996).

Christophe Schulte, *Zimzum: God and the Origin of the World* (University of Pennsylvania Press, 2023).

Maurice Blanchot, *Le pas au-delà* (Gallimard, 1973), 76.

Frag. 132

Klibansky, Panofsky, and Saxl, *Saturn and Melancholy,* 255, 258.

"Negative Senex and a Renaissance Solution," in *The Uniform Edition of the Writings of James Hillman,* vol. 3: *Senex & Puer,* edited by Glen Slater, (Spring Publications, 2021 [2005]).

Frag. 137

ὁδός ἄνω κάτω μία καὶ ὠυτή; Heraclitus, *Fragments,* edited and translated by T. M. Robinson (University of Toronto Press, 1987), frag. 60.

Frag. 142

Aletha Hayter, *Opium and the Romantic Imagination* (University of California Press, 1970)

Mathias Enard, *Boussole* (Actes Sud, 2015).

Frag. 144

Porphyry, *On the Cave of the Nymphs,* translated by Robert Lamberton (Station Hill Press, 1983).

Homer, *Odyssey* 13.102–12.

Frag. 146

Marsilio Ficino, *De triplici vita* 3.14–20.

Frag. 149

Jacob Boehme, *Von der Gnadenwahl* [1623], edited by Gerhard Wehr (Insel Verlag, 1995).

C.G. Jung, "Der Geist Mercurius," *Eranos Yearbook* 9 (1942).

Paul F. Cowlan, *The Alchemical Mercurius* (Alembic, 2009).

Sean J. McGrath, *Thinking Nature: An Essay on Negative Ecology* (Edinburgh University Press, 2019).

Frag. 155

John Keats, "Ode to a Nightingale," *www.poetryfoundation.org/poems/44479/ode-to-a-nightingale.*

G.W.F. Hegel, *The Phenomenology of Spirit*, translated by Terry Pinkard (Cambridge University Press, 2018), 387 (par. 668).

Clark Lawlor, *Consumption and Literature: The Making of a Romantic Disease* (Palgrave-Macmillan, 2007).

Frag. 160

Thomas Mann, *Doktor Faustus* (1947).

Michel de Certeau, "Extase blanche," in *La faiblesse de croire* (Collection Esprit/Seuil, 1987), 315–18.

Maurice Boutin, "Finitude et transcendance: Conditions d'un changement de paradigm," in *Théologie négative*, edited by Marco M. Olivetti,(CEDAM, 2002), 341–55

Frag. 161

Sean McGrath, *The Dark Ground of Spirit: Schelling and the Unconscious* (Routledge, 2012), 120–79.

Frag. 162

Emanuel Swedenborg's *Journal of Dreams and Spiritual Exercises*, translated by C.T. Odhner (The Academy Book Room, 1918), 14, 100–101.

Frag. 165

Adrien Baillet, *La Vie de Monsieur Des-Cartes*, 2 vols. (Daniel Horthemels, 1691), 1: 78–86.

"Remarques sur l'abregé de la vie de Mons. des Cartes," in *Die Philosophische Schriften von Gottfried Wilhelm Leibniz*, edited by C.J. Gerhardt (Weidmansche Buchhandlung, 1880), 4: 315.

Frag. 166

Apeliotes is the Greek god of the Southeast wind—the right side when one faces north. Associated with spring rains, he is often depicted wearing boots and carrying fruit. Jupiter, king of the heavens, unity of the gods, throws thunderbolts. Hamlet was a bookish sort with a passion for the stage, and has trouble distinguishing between life and literature.

Frag. 168

René Descartes, *Mediations on First Philosophy*, translated by John Cottingham (Cambridge University Press, 1996), First Meditation, 12–15.

René Descartes, *A Discourse on the Method*, translated by Ian MacLean (Oxford University Press, 2006), Part Two, 12–20.

Frag. 169

Freud, "Some Dreams of Descartes': A letter to Maxime Leroy" [1929], in *The Standard Edition*, 21: 203–4

Freud, *The Interpretation of Dreams*, in *The Standard Edition*, 5: 444

Maxime Leroy, *Descartes: le philosophe aux masques*, 2 vols. (Les Éditions Rieder, 1929).

Michael Keevak, "Descartes's Dreams and Their Address for Philosophy," *Journal of the History of Ideas* 53, no. 3 (1992): 373–96

Susana Gómez López, "Enthusiasm and Platonic Furor in the Origins of Cartesian Science: The Olympian Dreams," *Early Science and Medicine* 25, no. 5 (2020): 507–35.

Frag. 170

Rainer Maria Rilke, "Du Dunkelheit, aus der ich stamme," in *Das Stundenbuch* [1899], 1: *Das Buch vom mönchischen Leben* (Insel-Verlag, 1905); my translation.

www.ingramcontent.com/pod-product-compliance
Lightning Source LLC
Chambersburg PA
CBHW031425150426
43191CB00006B/400